Study Guide

to accompany

Nash • Jeffrey
Howe • Frederick • Davis • Winkler

THE AMERICAN PEOPLE
Creating a Nation and a Society

Volume Two from 1865
Fourth Edition

Julie Roy Jeffrey
Goucher College

Peter J. Frederick
Wabash College

Neal A. Brooks
Essex Community College

Elizabeth M. Nix
Essex Community College

An Imprint of Addison Wesley Longman, Inc.

New York • Reading, Massachusetts • Menlo Park, California • Harlow, England
Don Mills, Ontario • Sydney • Mexico City • Madrid • Amsterdam

Study Guide to accompany Nash/Jeffrey/Howe/Frederick/Davis/Winkler, *The American People: Creating a Nation and a Society*, Fourth Edition, Volume II from 1865.

ISBN: 0-321-01635-1

CB

97 98 99 00 01 9 8 7 6 5 4 3 2 1

TABLE OF CONTENTS

"A people without history is like wind upon the buffalo grass."
—Lakota

Acknowledgments

Our ideas about teaching and learning have several sources, but none so important as those interactions and friendships with our students at Essex Community College and the University of Baltimore. From them we have learned to appreciate the trials and successes of students in an introductory history course. They have explained their dismay over the amount of material to read and digest, as well as the continual concern over which issues are most important. We thank our editors, Jessica Bayne and Jennifer McCaffery, at Addison Wesley Longman. Our colleague William C. Hughes has generously assisted with information from his extensive film data base. Special thanks are also due to Andrew Imparato for his editing and word processing skills, and to Susie Bane of Tech-Team in Timonium, Maryland, a former Essex student and talented word processor who assisted in the preparation of the fourth edition.

Neal A. Brooks/Elizabeth M. Nix

"The value of History is, indeed, not scientific but moral: by liberalizing the mind, by deepening the sympathies, by fortifying the will, it enables us to control, not society, but ourselves . . . and to meet the future."

—Carl L. Becker

INTRODUCTION

How to Do Well in Your History Course by Rediscovering the Past

In one of Garry Trudeau's "Doonesbury" cartoons, Mike and Zonker are strolling through the woods as Zonker reminisces about their college days. Among other things, he says, they went on study dates in the boat house, held midnight sledding parties, parked the dean's Volvo inside the chapel, got busted at a rock concert, and ran naked through a meeting of the board of trustees. After listening to Zonker's recollections of those "bright college years," Mike reminds him that "we never did any of those things." Zonker agrees, saying, "I know, but one day we'll think we did." "Isn't it a little early to start embellishing?" Mike asks. Zonker coolly responds, "You gotta grab the past while you can!"

We introduce the study guide to *The American People: Creating a Nation and a Society* with this cartoon for two reasons. First, we are aware that the conflicting demands and pressures of college life often lead students to pranks, pizza parlors, parties, and paper deadline panics—the kinds of events that stimulated Zonker's imagination. Exaggerated and embellished as his fantasies were, they suggest the range of experiences we know students go through, or think about, during their college years. We certainly did. Our current fantasy is that you might add the study of American history to the positive college experiences you will remember in later years—not made up, like Zonker's, but for real!

We have prepared this study guide, therefore, to smooth your way through the American history textbook, not as a substitute for it but as a supplement—a guide to reading *The American People* for maximum understanding, appreciation, enjoyment, and, yes, success on examinations. To be sure, you have many long hours of reading, reflection, and study ahead of you. Studying history is not easy. But it can be pleasurable as well as profitable, and we sincerely hope that you will find your study of American history almost as enjoyable—and certainly as educational—as the diversions that Zonker imagined as a college student.

We also introduce this guide with Trudeau's cartoon because the last lines say something significant not only about students but also about historians. Although professionally committed to telling the truth about the past, which for the most part they succeed in doing, historians tend sometimes, like Zonker, to "embellish." Like any good storytellers, historians enjoy building an exciting drama by the addition of juicy adjectives and heightened tension. Occasionally, they even get a date or name wrong. At one level this is inexcusable, and historians try to check and double-check their facts so as never to make errors. But they are only human, and both the authors of your textbook and your history professor may sometimes embellish or make mistakes. So will you, but your errors will be marked wrong. The ultimate responsibility for "getting the history right," therefore, is yours.

Historians also embellish when they interpret the past, not by telling inflated stories or committing factual errors but simply by showing their human point of view, which is the result of their particular time, place, circumstances, and personal backgrounds. Such factors influence the selection and interpretation of past events. Interpretation is unavoidable, and students should beware of a book or person that claims to be "the truth" rather than one interpretation of the truth.

All works of history, even textbooks, present a point of view reflecting the values, assumptions, and interests of the author. Interpretation differs from a biased presentation in that the latter willfully distorts truth while the former deepens understanding by the process of explaining how and why things happened in the past. This makes the writing (and teaching) of history more than a listing of names, dates, and other facts. The act of interpretation is a humble one, and you should be looking for the interpretive point of view of the authors of your textbook as you read. The Preface is a good place to start.

The history presented in *The American People* is enriched by an interpretive framework. It tells the story of the many ways in which the diverse people coming to this country—whether on the *Mayflower,* slave ships, immigrant steamers, Caribbean fishing boats, or rafts across the Rio Grande—created many societies and one nation. These individual stories make up the collective story of the American people. Our major goal is to help you both learn and enjoy this story of "the American people." In the 1990s, as we continue to seek to know who we are by knowing who we were, we realize that, like Michael Doonesbury, "you gotta grab the past while you can."

IMPORTANT ASSUMPTIONS TO BE AWARE OF

Toward that end, we have prepared this study guide. Your teacher has a similar one. We believe that you should know some of our most important assumptions as we prepared the textbook and these guides. They are as follows:

1. The authors have tried to write a textbook that is not just a series of historical names, dates, places, and other facts—"one damned thing after another," as someone once described history. Rather, we show history as a story of the daily lives of both ordinary and famous Americans in the past. We have sought to take you inside these lives, to experience the fears, frustrations, and aspirations of the American people.

2. We want you not only to reexperience these lives but also to be confident that you remember what you have studied. When learning history is connected to your own experiences, as well as fun, you tend to do better on tests.

3.   We believe that the textbook and guides are only as good as they are teachable and learnable. We have designed both the text and these guides to be immediately usable, if a teacher desires, for a variety of classroom learning activities and assignments that enrich student learning and the appreciation of American history.

4.   We believe that students—all people, in fact—learn best when they begin with a personally compelling human experience, their own or someone else's. This human story suggests further stories, or facts, and some overarching themes and concepts. These are in turn analyzed, interpreted, compared to other facts, applied to other settings, and evaluated. Finally, there must be an opportunity to express what one has learned and to receive feedback on how well. We have structured the textbook and this guide according to this basic pattern of human learning.

HOW TO UNDERSTAND A CHAPTER

Take Chapter 17, for example, which begins with the story of two families who settled in Nebraska in the 1870s. Both experience natural disasters and hardships. Hattie Leeper dies in childbirth and her survivors leave their claim. The Ebbesens, Danish immigrants, weather the challenges more successfully, but they eagerly sell their homestead after a devastating hailstorm. Like many other agrarians of this period, they too leave their farm and move to town.

These two stories introduce most of the overarching themes and major concepts of Chapter 17 and, indeed, of agrarian life in the post - Civil War era. Their attempts and failures point to the difficulties farmers had in realizing the traditional dream of rural independence and prosperity. As the nation's economy matured and power permanently left the farm lands, agrarian Americans had to adjust. The responses of Native Americans, African-Americans, southerners and midwestern farmers like the Leepers and the Ebbesns are the important themes of this chapter. The fact that the chapter opens with the tales of these families demonstrates the emphasis of the lives of ordinary people rather than on national politics that we make in this particular chapter and in the text as a whole. It is therefore important to pay special attention to the elements of each opening anecdote to see how the story reveals the keys to the major themes of the chapter.

The bedrock of history, as history students have found out, often to their despair, is composed of facts. Broad historical themes are the handles, or pegs, upon which to hang the many particular facts that make up the past. These facts must be mastered—often by memorization—in order to provide life and substance to the larger themes. In Chapter 16, for example, there are a number of names, dates, places, and terms. But once you are familiar with major concepts like the basic goals and interactions of three groups and the ways in which their dreams conflicted, the facts can be placed in some category, or hung on some peg, and are therefore easier to remember. Think, for example, of how you would categorize and remember such particular facts and terms as bonanza farms, the ghost dance, the New South, the Dawes Act, the Grange, the Ocala Platform, Jim Crow laws, and the Compromise of 1877.

Once the facts are mastered within the context of the major themes, you are able to work with, or use, both facts and concepts in a more sophisticated way than just repeating or listing them. You could, for example, analyze the motivations behind the goals of each group, showing the roots of these goals and the reasons why they came into conflict. Or you could assess how well each group achieved its goals. Or you could apply or transfer your knowledge about the changes that took place in America as it moved from an agrarian to an industrial economy to the changes taking place today as we move from an industrial to an information age. If so, you might evaluate the similarities and differences that are suggested about the way Americans adapt to change, whom they bulldoze and whom they scapegoat. Being able to form larger judgments like these is the highest level of learning and can only follow—indeed, depends on—prior understanding of specific facts and thematic concepts.

Finally, to check how well you have learned the material of a chapter, it is good to be tested—on both the specific facts and the larger themes of that chapter. This feedback is necessary both to confirm your confidence in how much has been learned and to identify areas that need further study.

To summarize, most people learn best by moving through the following sequence:

1. Engagement in a human story
2. An overview of major themes and concepts
3. Mastery of specific facts that support or illustrate those themes
4. Analysis, synthesis, comparison, application, and evaluation of the themes
5. An opportunity to demonstrate knowledge by practicing these steps on tests and other assignments

Each chapter in *The American People* can be understood better by studying it in terms of this basic learning pattern. We have also included summaries of the major parts of the text and three "technological innovations" to enhance your historical understanding.

HOW TO USE THE STUDY GUIDE WITH THE TEXT

The study guide also follows this pattern. Students who work back and forth from the chapter in *The American People* to the chapter in the guide will continually be reinforcing and strengthening their mastery and enjoyment of American history. With a little experimenting, students will find that it is sometimes better to read the textbook chapter before looking at the guide and sometimes better to read the guide before the textbook.

Each chapter contains the following sections:

(1) Chapter Outline (with opening anecdote)

It is helpful to look through the outline before reading a chapter in order to see at a glance both the major topics to be covered and the chapter's organization. The short summary of the human story or anecdote that begins each chapter should point toward these topics and suggest the structure.

(2) Significant Themes and Highlights

Three or four statements will provide an overview summary of the main themes, concepts, threads, major ideas, and special features of each chapter. To consult this section before reading the chapter may be the most helpful thing you can do in order to have some handles or pegs to help you understand and place the many particular facts encountered in the chapter. Keeping these major concepts in mind as you read will prevent you from getting lost in a sea of facts. Specific facts are valuable to a historian only as illustrations of some larger theme. If you have a strong sense of the themes, you will more easily remember the appropriate illustrative factual examples when taking examinations.

(3) Learning Goals

The list of the goals, or objectives, of each chapter is a way of providing a self-check on how well you are mastering the material. After completing a chapter, try answering each item. If you can, you are ready to move on. If you cannot, you know which topics to review in the chapter. When you are preparing for examinations, reread the sections on learning goals for the appropriate chapters.

The first five or six learning goals indicate the "basic knowledge" you should be familiar with—the essential facts every history student has to know before doing anything else. Such knowledge is usually tested with short-answer exam questions: multiple-choice, true-or-false, identification, fill-in-the-blanks, and similar formats. You also need to know these facts in order to handle more difficult kinds of questions. The second part of the learning goals section includes three goals intended to give you "Practice in Historical Thinking Skills," higher-order learning tasks such as analyzing, comparing and contrasting, applying, assessing, and evaluating historical phenomena. This is what we mean by interpretation. These intellectual skills are usually tested by essay questions and paper assignments. You can prepare for these by writing short practice essays on these three learning goals.

(4) Important Dates and Names to Know

Nothing drives history students crazier than having to memorize dates. Yet chronology, the order and sequence of past events, is essential to understanding history. What is most important for students to remember is not that they must memorize every exact date but rather that they should form a general idea of the sequence in which events happened. Remembering key dates is not as mysterious as students often think; it is usually just a matter of common sense. One could, for example, remember that the Declaration of Independence was signed in 1776 and the Constitution in 1787, but what is really important is to get them in the right order. Imagine how silly it would be to reverse them. It is common sense that the bonds of one government had to be dissolved before a new one could be created. The chronologies of important dates will usually include important names to remember as well. Names that are not associated with a particular date but are nevertheless significant are listed at the end of the chronology.

(5) Glossary of Important Terms

Although history is not nearly as filled with jargon and special vocabularies as other disciplines, various unfamiliar terms inevitably turn up in every chapter. These are listed and briefly identified in this section. Remember that your teachers may also have favorite terms that they want you to learn, so it is a good idea to add them to these lists.

(6) Enrichment Ideas

We think this is the most important section in the guides. In this part is a list of activities and assignments designed to aid and enhance learning of the important themes and concepts in each chapter. Some are activities you can follow and do on your own. A longer list, not included in the student guide, contains assignments and classroom activities your instructor may want to use. The variety of suggested approaches to enrich learning—both in the classroom and out—is extensive, but they always begin with further ways of using the "Recovering the Past" feature. This section, found in each chapter, is intended to introduce students of history to the many sources and ways in which historians find out what happened in the past.

A century ago, most historians would probably have said that they recovered the past by reading old manuscripts, primarily government and other institutional documents housed in official archives, and by consulting the letters, papers, and manuscripts of former presidents, senators, generals, and other leaders. But in recent years, as historians have broadened their interest from political and military history (unkindly called "drum and trumpets" history) to include the social history of ordinary people, they have also widened the kinds of sources they find useful in recovering the past. To written government documents and archival manuscripts historians have added private diaries, popular songs, paintings, cartoons, census returns, tax and inventory lists, films and photographs, material objects, oral history, and many other means of recovering the past.

The "RTPs," as the authors affectionately call them, are intended not only to enrich your learning of American history but also to show how you can become your own historian. For the most part, each means of recovering the past is appropriate to the content of the chapter in which it is found. Thus the work of archaeologists and the contributions archaeology makes to understanding earlier civilizations are discussed in Chapter 1; folktales in the chapter on slavery; and films, oral history, and television in the twentieth-century chapters. Additional ways of recovering the past, such as popular Hollywood feature films and trips to historical areas, are mentioned in the appropriate Enrichment sections in the study guide.

(7) Sample Test and Examination Questions

Many students will find this section most useful in preparing for examinations, not because their teachers will necessarily select test questions from those included (though they might) but because students can check for themselves how well they have learned the material in a chapter. Note that the sample questions begin with short-answer types (multiple choice, matching, etc.) to test basic knowledge (how well you remember the material), whereas the later questions are essays and interpretive questions that test historical thinking skills (how well you can compare and contrast, analyze, interpret, apply, and evaluate the main ideas of the chapter). In these higher-order questions, you gain practice in learning how to think like historians, doing the kind of basic detective groundwork interpreting evidence from various sources and writing analytic essays.

The test questions for some chapters in this guide end with a map question, which is a lower-order but important content knowledge skill (knowing where places are). Other chapters end with a quotation, chart, or other verbal or quantitative illustration, which we ask you to identify and interpret—who, what, where, when, and why. This is a more sophisticated exercise in the detection and interpretation of a historical source.

HOW TO UNDERLINE A CHAPTER

One of the first problems students face when they begin reading a textbook is how much to underline or highlight. A consideration of the purpose of underlining may help guide you through a chapter. The major goal, of course, is to aid memory and comprehension by highlighting the main themes, selecting important examples for each major idea. This helps not only to understand the chapter but also to review for examinations. Too little underlining means that you may end up rereading the entire chapter the night before a test. Too much, in which no discrimination has taken place, may also mean having to reread everything. It is, of course, important to note the topic sentences for each paragraph. In addition, pay particular attention to the one or two paragraphs that make the transition from the opening anecdote to the main body of the chapter. These state the major themes and often even the organization of the chapter.

The following shows an example of how we would underline the transition paragraph and a short section from Chapter 17.

The story of the Leepers and the Ebbesens, though different in their details and endings, hints at some of the <u>problems confronting rural Americans in the last quarter of the nineteenth century</u>. As a mature <u>industrial economy transformed agriculture and shifted the balance of economic power</u> permanently away from America's farmlands to the country's cities and factories, <u>many farmers found it impossible to realize the traditional dream of rural independence and prosperity</u>. Even bountiful harvests no longer guaranteed success. "We were told two years ago to go to work and raise a big crop; that was all we needed," said one farmer. "We went to work and plowed and planted; the rains fell, the sun shone, nature smiled, and we raised the big crop they told us to; and what came of it? Eight cents corn, ten cent oats, two cent beef and no price at all for butter and eggs — that's what came of it." <u>Native Americans also discovered that changes in rural life threatened their values and dreams</u>. As the Sioux leader Red Cloud told railroad surveyors in Wyoming, "We do not want you here. You are scaring away the buffalo."

This chapter explores the <u>agricultural transformation</u> of the late nineteenth century and highlights the ways in which rural Americans—red, white, and black—joined the industrial world and responded to new conditions. The <u>rise of large-scale agriculture in the West and the development of the Great Plains</u> form a backdrop for the discussion of the <u>impact of white settlement on western tribes</u> and their reactions to white incursions. In an analysis of the South, the <u>efforts of whites to create a "New South" form a contrast to the underlying realities of race and cotton</u>. While the chapter shows that <u>discrimination and economic peonage</u> characterize the lives of <u>most black southerners during</u> this period, it also describes the rise of new black protest tactics and ideologies. Finally, the chapter also highlights the ways in which agricultural problems of the late nineteenth century, which would continue to characterize much of agricultural life in the twentieth century, <u>led American farmers to protest their place in American life and to form the Populist party</u>.

The White Perspective

<u>At the end of the Civil War, a state of war existed between red and white men on the Plains</u>. The shameful massacre of friendly Cheyenne at Sand Creek, Colorado, by the Colorado Volunteers in 1864 sparked widespread hostilities. Although not all whites condoned the slaughter, the deliberations of the <u>congressional commission</u> authorized to make peace on the Plains illustrated the limits of their point of view. The commission, which included the commander of the Army in the West, Civil War hero General William T. Sherman, accepted as fact that "an industrious, thrifty, and enlightened population" of whites would occupy most of the West. <u>All Native Americans</u>, the commission believed, <u>should relocate</u> in one of two areas: the western half of present-day South Dakota, or Oklahoma. There they would <u>learn the ways of white society and "civilized" life</u>.

At two major conferences in <u>1867</u> and <u>1868, Native American chiefs</u> listened to these proposals. <u>Some agreed with the terms; others did not</u>. As Satanta, a Kiowa chief explained, "I don't want to settle. I love to roam over the prai-

ries." In any case, the agreements extracted were not binding since none of the chiefs had authority to speak for their tribes. The U.S. Senate dragged its feet in approving the treaties. <u>Supplies promised to Indians</u> who settled in the reserved areas <u>failed to materialize</u>, and wildlife proved too sparse to support them. These Indians soon drifted back to their former hunting grounds.

As General Sherman had warned, however, "All who cling to their old hunting ground are hostile and will remain so till killed off." To his brother he had written, "The more we can kill this year, the less will have to be killed the next war."

8

AN INDUSTRIALIZING PEOPLE
1865 - 1900

In the last quarter of the nineteenth century, with the mixed legacy of Reconstruction laying the groundwork for a century more of black struggle, described in Chapter 16, Americans turned their energies toward transforming their society from one based on agriculture to one based on heavy industry. This economic and social transition was neither smooth nor steady. But by 1900, the United States had emerged as one of the world's great industrial powers.

Chapters 17, 18, and 19 form a unit. Chapter 17, "The Farmer's World," examines the ways in which American farmers modernized and vastly expanded production after the Civil War. Even though agriculture provided the basis for urban industrial development, many farmers did not win the rewards they had anticipated. The South remained backward despite efforts to modernize. Rural protest publicized farmers' complaints and contributed to the formation of a powerful third party. While the postwar period was difficult for some farmers, it was disastrous for Native Americans. By 1900, the power of the Plains Indians had been broken and the reservation system finally set in place.

Chapter 18, "The Rise of Smokestack America," focuses on the character of industrial progress and urban expansion. We explore the growing diversity of the American work force and middle classes and the various experiences in and responses to the new world of industry. The labor conflicts of the period indicate the difficulty of these years for most working class Americans.

In Chapter 19, "Politics and Reform," we see how the national politics of the Gilded Age largely ignored the needs of farmers, workers, and other ordinary Americans. But with the increasing role of middle-class reformers, and with the stark inequalities of wealth as dramatized by the Populist revolt and depression of 1893 - 1897, the 1890s were a turning point in American attitudes and political party alignments.

Chapter 20, "Becoming a World Power," demonstrates the international consequences of the country's successful industrialization and its emerging sense of national identity and power. Like other world powers, the United States nourished imperial ambitions in the 1890s and acquired its own colonies. But expansionism brought difficult dilemmas and tensions in America's relationship with the rest of the world. After 1900, the United States continued to play an active role in the events and affairs of Europe and Asia and especially in Central America and the Caribbean.

17

The Farmer's World

(1) CHAPTER OUTLINE

Hattie and Milton Leeper work to establish themselves on the Nebraska frontier. They win a modest prosperity before Hattie dies in childbirth and Milton leaves the family claim. The Ebbesens, a Danish family, face natural disasters, but they survive and establish themselves in some comfort in a Nebraska town.

Modernizing Agriculture
    Rural Myth and Reality
    New Farmers, New Farms
    Overproduction and Falling Prices
    Farming on the Western Plains, 1880s - 1890s
    The Early Cattle Frontier, 1860 - 1890
    Cornucopia on the Pacific
    Exploiting Natural Resources

The Second Great Removal
    Background to Hostilities
    The White Perspective
    The Tribal View
    The Dawes Act, 1887
    The Ghost Dance: An Indian Renewal Ritual

The New South
    Postwar Southerners Face the Future
    The Other Side of Progress
    Cotton Still King
    The Nadir of Black Life
    Diverging Black Responses

Farm Protest
    The Grange in the 1860s and 1870s
    The Interstate Commerce Act, 1887
    The Southern Farmers' Alliance in the 1880s and 1890s
    The Ocala Platform, 1890
    The People's Party, 1892

Conclusion: Farming in the Industrial Age

(2) SIGNIFICANT THEMES AND HIGHLIGHTS

1. This chapter focuses on rural America, where, like the Leepers and Ebbesens, the majority of Americans lived between 1865 and 1900. The chapter shows the economic changes of the post - Civil War period: machinery became increasingly necessary, farm operations brought new lands into use, and regional diversification and crop specialization came to characterize American agriculture. The chapter shows the impact of these changes on American farmers and stresses the significance of falling prices and overproduction.

2. The theme of racial conflict on the Plains frontier continues from the perspective of both white Americans and Native Americans. Black Elk, an Ogalala Sioux holy man, provides an example of the Native American perspective as the reservation policy reaches maturity.

3. The chapter explores the meaning of the "New South," contrasting the reality of northern control, the continuing dominance of cotton, and widespread poverty with the dreams and goals of New South spokesmen. The hardening of racial attitudes in the New South is described along with black reactions.

4. Farm protest movements (the Grange and the Southern Farmers' Alliance) are explained as responses to new conditions, though not always entirely rational ones. The interest in collective solutions in the Southern Alliance suggests a link with the labor protest described in Chapter 18. Although the rural discontent is highlighted here, the majority of rural Americans did not participate in overt protest movements.

(3) LEARNING GOALS

Familiarity with Basic Knowledge

After reading this chapter, you should be able to:

1. List four ways in which farmers responded to the new conditions of the post - Civil War period.

2. Describe three ways in which the development of the Plains frontier was linked to technological advances.

3. Identify the steps leading to the Dawes Act and describe its terms.

4. Explain the goals of New South spokesmen and contrast the realities of industrial and agricultural development with these goals.

5. Describe the steps stripping blacks of their political rights and the implementation of "Jim Crow" laws, and outline the various black responses.

6. List the major planks of the Ocala Platform in 1890 and of the Omaha Platform in 1892.

Practice in Historical Thinking Skills

After reading this chapter, you should be able to:

1. Discuss the ways in which the Southern Farmers' Alliance represented a more comprehensive approach to the problems of the American farmer than that developed by the Grange.

2. Explain why the 1890s has been called the nadir of black status in the South.

3. Discuss the importance of populism in terms of rural protest and political debate.

(4) IMPORTANT DATES AND NAMES TO KNOW

1860s	Cattle drives from Texas begin
1865 - 1867	Sioux Wars on the Great Plains
1867	National Grange founded
1869	Transcontinental railroad completed
1869 - 1874	Granger laws
1873	Financial panic triggers economic depression
1874	Barbed wire patented
1875	Black Hills gold rush incites Sioux War
1876	Custer's last stand at Little Bighorn
1877	*Munn* v. *Illinois* Bonanza farms in the Great Plains
1878	Timber and Stone Act
1880s	"New South"
1881	Tuskegee Institute founded

1883 - 1885	Depression
1884	Southern Farmers' Alliance founded
1886	Severe winter ends cattle boom *Wabash* v. *Illinois*
1887	Dawes Severalty Act Interstate Commerce Act Farm prices plummet
1888	Colored Farmers' Alliance founded
1890	Afro-American League founded Sioux Ghost Dance movement Massacre at Wounded Knee Ocala Platform Yosemite National Park established
1890s	Black disfranchisement in South Jim Crow laws passed in South Declining farm prices
1891	Forest Reserve Act
1892	Populist party formed Sierra Club founded
1895	Booker T. Washington's "Atlanta Compromise" address
1896	*Plessy* v. *Ferguson*

Other Names to Know

Henry Grady	Black Elk
W. E. B. Du Bois	James B. Weaver
Ida B. Wells	Wovoka
John Muir	Sitting Bull

(5) GLOSSARY OF IMPORTANT TERMS

Jim Crow laws: state and local laws mandating the separation of whites and blacks; this legal segregation is often called de jure segregation (segregation by law) while informal segregation is called de facto segregation (segregation in practice)

deflation: falling prices

poll tax: a tax that had to be paid in order to vote; this device was used in the South to exclude poor black and white voters

(6) ENRICHMENT IDEAS

1. Recovering The Past for this chapter deals with middle-class journals published in the nineteenth century. College and university libraries often have at least some of these journals in their collections. See what your library has. You might want to look through the issues for one of the years discussed in this chapter. What seems to be the major topic of interest in the journals you have chosen? What are the controversial issues? Do the journals deal with any of the events covered here? If so, what are the main points of the discussion? The point of view? Is there much sympathy for the problems of farmers, Indians, or blacks? There are many questions that you might want to ask, depending on your source.

2. Although the film *Heartland* presents the frontier in a slightly later period, it is worth seeing for the picture it gives of frontier life, and in particular a woman's response to frontier conditions. The film is available on videotape.

3. Many novels and books of general interest deal with some of the topics of this chapter—in particular, life on the Plains frontier and the struggle between the Plains Indians and whites. Examples of vivid novels are Hamlin Garland, *Main-Travelled Roads* (1891); Frank Norris, *The Octopus* (1901); Willa Cather, *O Pioneers!* (1913); and Ole Rolvaag, *Giants in the Earth* (1927). They present many different points of view that you will want to consider.

4. Letters and diaries written by foreign immigrants on the Plains frontier can be found in published form and in local historical societies. They offer an interesting perspective on the frontier experience. Older residents of communities in this region of the country still remember information on frontier life from relatives and family. You could interview some of these residents.

5. Read William Faulkner's short novel *The Bear*. How does it trace the changes taking place in the New South? How do whites, blacks, and Native Americans interact? Do you read it as history or allegory?

6. *All God's Dangers* is a fascinating oral history about the life of Nate Shaw, a black sharecropper in the South involved in the agrarian labor movement. Read all or parts of it to discover Shaw's way with words, priorities, struggles, and achievements.

(7) SAMPLE TEST AND EXAMINATION QUESTIONS

Multiple choice: Choose the best answer.

1. American farmers
   a. saw little conflict between rural America and the technological industrial world
   b. thought that farming was not a business
   c. were convinced that they should cut back production
   d. were heartened by the rising prices for their products

2. All of the following are true about the Plains frontier EXCEPT that it
   a. attracted large numbers of immigrants
   b. would not have been developed without the technological improvements of the age
   c. demanded resourcefulness on the part of settlers
   d. had ample rainfall during the 1880s and 1890s

3. Most Plains farmers
   a. were tenants
   b. took up land under the Homestead Act
   c. bought land outright
   d. were squatters

4. California farms in the nineteenth century were
   a. larger than the national average
   b. of average size
   c. smaller than the national average
   d. collectivized by the state

5. The cattle frontier
   a. was profitable because cattle could graze on public lands
   b. rewarded cowboys handsomely for their work
   c. was successful because of careful breeding
   d. was not particularly profitable because longhorn cattle were not very good for eating

6. Efforts to "solve" the Indian question
   a. bore little relation to the completion of the transcontinental railroad
   b. had as a basic assumption that Indians must learn white ways of life
   c. effectively halted the slaughter of the buffalo
   d. were scrupulous in respecting Indian rights to their lands

7. New South spokesmen

a. urged the South to increase the production of cotton
b. believed that it was important for the South to be self-sufficient
c. rejected entrepreneurial values
d. rejected northern dollars for southern development

8. Southern industrial workers
   a. included large numbers of women and children
   b. earned wages similar to those of their northern counterparts
   c. worked about the same number of hours as their northern counterparts
   d. included a high percentage of blacks

9. In the New South,
   a. farmers diversified their crops
   b. sharecropping ended
   c. the dominance of cotton continued
   d. land ownership became increasingly widespread

10. The 1896 Supreme Court decision of *Plessy* v. *Ferguson*
    a. took a strong stand against the trend toward segregation in the South
    b. came out in favor of "separate but equal" facilities in the South
    c. declared the poll tax illegal
    d. came out against trusts

11. Booker T. Washington
    a. argued that the problem of the twentieth century would be that of the color line
    b. advocated black militancy
    c. was not interested in the struggle for black social and political equality
    d. was unpopular among white leaders

12. The Grange
    a. developed a sophisticated analysis of the ills of American agriculture
    b. blamed the railroads, middlemen, and elevator operators for their difficulties
    c. did not believe in cooperatives
    d. was only a social organization

13. The Interstate Commerce Commission
    a. lacked enforcement power
    b. regulated railroad rates effectively
    c. was supported by a series of court decisions
    d. was honored by businessmen

14. The Southern Farmers' Alliance was characterized by all of the following EXCEPT
    a. a network of Alliance lecturers

b. cooperative buying and selling exchanges
c. a position advocating an increased supply of money
d. an all-male membership policy

15. Populist supporters included
    a. most rural Americans
    b. city workers
    c. farmers living in isolated rural areas
    d. only the poorest and most debt-ridden farmers

16. The Populist party was perceived by many Americans as
    a. just another party
    b. a radical threat to the established order
    c. a splinter group of the Republican party
    d. a rational response to new conditions

17. The late nineteenth century was a period of
    a. falling prices
    b. stable prices
    c. rising prices
    d. an increasing supply of money

Identify and show a relationship between each of the following pairs:

Jim Crow laws	*and*	the Dawes Act
Henry Grady	*and*	Leonidas Polk
Booker T. Washington	*and*	*Plessy* v. *Ferguson*
the Knights of Labor	*and*	the New South
Wounded Knee	*and*	the Ghost Dance movement

Essays

1. Develop as essays items 2 and 3 from "Practice in Historical Thinking Skills" in the "Learning Goals" section.

2. The American farmers' problems stemmed from their success at adapting to the modern industrial world. Develop an essay that discusses this statement.

3. The clash between the Plains Indians, white settlers, and the U.S. Army was intimately tied to the economic transformation of the post - Civil War era. In what ways is this statement accurate?

Identify and Interpret: Quotation
(that is, state who, what, where, when, and why significant)

The wisest among my race understand that the agitation of questions of social equality is the extremest folly, and that progress in the enjoyment of all the privileges that will come to us must be the result of severe and constant struggle rather than of artificial forcing. No race that has anything to contribute to the markets of the world is long in any degree ostracized. It is important and right that all privileges of the law be ours, but it is vastly more important that we be prepared for the exercise of these privileges. The opportunity to earn a dollar in a factory just now is worth infinitely more than the opportunity to spend a dollar in an opera-house.

18

The Rise of Smokestack America

(1) CHAPTER OUTLINE

Thomas O'Donnell's testimony highlights the marginal existence of many working-class Americans in the late nineteenth century. The responses of congressional committee members to his story show that they are far more familiar with the fruits of industrial progress than with its underside.

The Texture of Industrial Progress
> The Rise of Heavy Industry from 1880 to 1900
> Financing Postwar Growth
> Railroads: Pioneers of Big Business
> Growth in Other Industries
> The Erratic Economic Cycle
> Pollution

Urban Expansion in the Industrial Age
> A Growing Population
> American Urban Dwellers
> The New Immigration, 1880 - 1900
> The Industrial City, 1880 - 1900
> Neighborhoods and Neighborhood Life
> Streetcar Suburbs
> The Social Geography of the Cities

The Life of the Middle Class
> New Freedoms for Middle-Class Women
> Male Mobility and the Success Ethic

Industrial Work and the Laboring Class
> The Impact of Ethnic Diversity
> The Changing Nature of Work
> Work Settings and Experiences
> The Worker's Share in Industrial Progress
> The Family Economy
> Women at Work

Capital Versus Labor
   On-the-Job Protests
   Strike Activity After 1876
   Labor Organizing, 1865 - 1900
   The Knights of Labor and the AFL
   Working-Class Setbacks
   The Homestead and Pullman Strikes of 1892 and 1894
   The Balance Sheet

Conclusion: The Complexity of Industrial Capitalism

(2) SIGNIFICANT THEMES AND HIGHLIGHTS

1. This chapter examines America's industrial transformation between 1865 and 1900 and highlights its special characteristics. The importance of big business, the rise of heavy industry, rapid urbanization, and the growth of an industrial work force are described as well as the unpredictable nature of the economic cycle and its impact on life. The testimony of Thomas O'Donnell reveals how one working-class American family fared in this period.

2. The chapter outlines the changing physical and social arrangements of the late nineteenth century and the varied living and working conditions for its different groups. In most cities, people were separated by class, ethnicity, and occupation, which often led to social distance, ignorance, prejudice, and sometimes even violence.

3. The world of work and its mixed blessings and burdens are described for working-class and middle-class Americans.

4. The various conflicts between capital and labor provide the material for the chapter's conclusion. Several of the major strikes are analyzed in detail, although the chapter emphasizes why most working-class Americans did not support unions.

(3) LEARNING GOALS

Familiarity with Basic Knowledge

After reading this chapter, you should be able to:

1. List three ways in which big business contributed to economic growth and three reasons why big business contributed to economic instability.

2. Describe the physical and social arrangements of the industrial city and neighborhood life.

3. Describe important changes in middle-class life.

4. Show how late-nineteenth-century industrialism changed the composition of the work force and state why working-class Americans often had to depend on the labor of their children.

5. Point out the different positions taken by workers on the pace of production, individualism, and union activity.

6. Describe two major incidents of working-class activism and their outcomes.

Practice in Historical Thinking Skills

After reading this chapter, you should be able to:

1. Discuss the extent and importance of occupational mobility for the American working class.

2. Explain why working-class Americans were often reluctant to join unions.

3. Discuss the role ethnicity played in working-class life.

(4) IMPORTANT DATES AND NAMES TO KNOW

1844 - 1884   "Old immigration"

1844   Telegraph invented

1850s   Steam power widely used in manufacturing

1859   Value of U.S. industrial production exceeds value of agricultural production

1866   National Labor Union founded

1869   Transcontinental railroad completed
               Knights of Labor organized

1870   Standard Oil of Ohio formed

1870s - 1880s Consolidation of continental railroad network

1873	Bethlehem Steel begins using Bessemer process
1873 - 1879	Depression
1876	Alexander Graham Bell invents telephone Thomas Edison establishes invention factory at Menlo Park, NJ
1877	Railroad workers hold first nationwide industrial strike
1879	Thomas Edison invents incandescent light
1882	Chinese Exclusion Act
1885 - 1914	"New immigration"
1886	American Federation of Labor (AFL) founded Haymarket Riot in Chicago
1887	Interstate Commerce Act
1890	Sherman Anti-Trust Act
1892	Standard Oil of New Jersey formed Coeur d'Alene strike Homestead steelworkers strike
1893	Chicago World's Fair
1893 - 1897	Depression
1894	Pullman railroad workers strike
1900	International Ladies' Garment Workers Union founded Corporations responsible for two-thirds of U.S. manufacturing

Other Names to Know

Samuel Gompers   Andrew Carnegie
Terence Powderly   John D. Rockefeller
Eugene Debs

(5) GLOSSARY OF IMPORTANT TERMS

pool: informal agreement between businessmen to stabilize business conditions by dividing the market or establishing uniform prices

rebate: a discount or partial return

horizontal integration: the growth of big business by combining similar businesses in order to gain a monopoly of the market

vertical integration: growth of big business by combining different stages of the production process to achieve economies of scale and independence from suppliers

strikebreaker: worker (often black or foreign) hired by owners to break a strike and undermine unions

(6) ENRICHMENT IDEAS

1. Using the Recovering the Past directions as a beginning, seek out material about late-nineteenth-century life by reading selected congressional hearings. What kinds of people are called upon to give testimony? How do congressional committee members respond to their testimony? Do you think there is much sympathy for the situation of working-class Americans?

2. What might a union organizer say to persuade the steelworkers that it was in their best interest to join the union? What might the responses be from each of the various ethnic groups in that community? From the native-born Americans? How might the managers respond?

3. Imagine yourself to be an immigrant from eastern Europe who has come to the United States for work. If you were to write a letter to relatives at home, would you tell them to join you or not? What would some of your comments be about housing, work, and opportunity?

4. Some of your relatives may well have migrated to this country in the early years of this century. Ask your grandparents and parents. This offers an excellent opportunity for an oral history as well as an investigation of family mementos and photographs.

(7) SAMPLE TEST AND EXAMINATION QUESTIONS

Multiple choice: Choose the best answer.

1. The introduction of the Bessemer process in the steel industry resulted in all of the following EXCEPT
   a. lower steel prices
   b. the continued use of iron rails
   c. the increasing use of steel for buildings
   d. more wire, nails, bolts, and screws

2. The rise of big business contributed to growth despite
   a. high fixed costs
   b. noncompetitive behavior
   c. poor management
   d. the stock market

3. Industrial growth was concentrated most dramatically in
   a. textiles
   b. metals
   c. machinery
   d. all of the above

4. The corporate form of organization was attractive to business for all of the following reasons EXCEPT
   a. it established a legal identity
   b. it provided investors with limited liability
   c. it did not protect investments
   d. Rockefeller liked it

5. The urban population explosion was due to
   a. the expanding size of American families
   b. a low urban death rate
   c. immigration
   d. mass black migration northward

6. Most foreign immigrants
   a. settled in New York City
   b. headed for the frontier
   c. went to the farms of the Midwest
   d. settled in cities

7. Middle-class women in the late nineteenth century
   a. used their new sense of freedom for both employment and many socially useful activities
   b. found easy acceptance in professional schools
   c. were so busy purchasing new products that they had no time for work or self-reflection
   d. won high paying jobs

8. Which of the following is not true? The occupational structure of the late nineteenth century
   a. bore no relation to ethnic origins
   b. was related to ethnic origins
   c. was related to race
   d. was related to gender

9. Industrial accident rates in the United States
   a. resembled those in other industrial countries
   b. were much lower than rates in other industrialized countries
   c. were much higher than rates in other industrialized countries
   d. were diminishing because of strict safety regulations

10. Most working-class Americans
    a. were skilled workers
    b. worked most of the year
    c. had steady pay
    d. frequently needed the wages of their children to survive

11. Women in the work force
    a. were most often in domestic service
    b. most often had factory jobs
    c. earned the same as men
    d. were almost always married

12. The Knights of Labor
    a. sought members only among skilled workers
    b. refused to accept women and blacks
    c. was open to all producers
    d. vigorously promoted strikes

13. Between 1870 and 1900, the percentage of workers in unions
    a. rose slightly
    b. declined dramatically
    c. declined slightly
    d. rose dramatically

14. According to the chapter author, the importance of the organization of workers
    a. lies in their triumph over capital
    b. stems from the rejection of the belief in individualism
    c. lies in their failure
    d. stems from their Marxist outlook

15. Most immigrants
    a. came with their families
    b. returned home after working for a few years
    c. came from the British Isles
    d. were young men of working age

Essays

1. Develop as essays items 1-3 under "Practice in Historical Thinking Skills" in the "Learning Goals" section.

2. Ethnicity bound American workers together at the same time that it prevented them from forming a united front against their bosses. Discuss the statement, giving suitable evidence.

3. Write an essay in which you show the ways in which the railroads became the prototype for late-nineteenth-century business.

4. Identify the chapter author's point of view about big business and working-class life in the late nineteenth century, and write an essay showing the extent to which you agree or disagree with it.

Identify and Interpret: Chart

(that is, first, study the chart and describe what it shows; second, analyze the chart by explaining some of the reasons behind the patterns you see; third, assess the larger significance of the chart)

WHITE FERTILITY RATES, 1800 - 1910

Year	*	Year	*	Year	*
1800	7.04	1840	6.14	1880	4.24
1810	6.92	1850	5.42	1890	3.87
1820	6.73	1860	5.21	1900	3.56
1830	6.55	1870	4.55	1910	3.42

Average number of live births per child-bearing woman.

19

Politics and Reform

(1) CHAPTER OUTLINE

Edward Bellamy's utopian novel *Looking Backward* contrasts the class divisions and competition of the nineteenth century with a harmonious, cooperative imaginary future society. The novel captures the fears and concerns of middle-class Americans as they struggled to cope with and reform an age marked by serious inequalities of wealth and political neglect.

Politics in the Gilded Age
Politics, Parties, Patronage, and Presidents
National Issues
The Lure of Local Politics

Middle-Class Reform
The Gospel of Wealth
Reform Darwinism and Pragmatism
Settlements and Social Gospel
Reforming the City
The Struggle for Women's Suffrage

The Pivotal 1890s
Republican Legislation in the Early 1890s
The Depression of 1893
The Crucial Election of 1896
The New Shape of American Politics

Conclusion: Looking Forward

(2) SIGNIFICANT THEMES AND HIGHLIGHTS

1. Bellamy's novel *Looking Backward* revealed the fears and concerns of many middle-class Americans as urbanization, industrial strife, and immigration changed the face of a once familiar America. The chapter describes the increasing attention of middle-class

reformers, many of them Christian intellectuals and women social settlement workers, to urban and other ills in American society. The most serious concern was the growing inequality of wealth, fictionalized in Bellamy's coach scene but actualized in the depression of the mid-1890s.

2. National politics, marked by high voter turnouts and locked in a stalemate between the two major parties, ignored the needs of farmers, workers, and other ordinary Americans, and did little to remedy inequalities of wealth. This chapter draws a sharp contrast between the issues faced (and ignored) at the national level and the lure of such issues as education, temperance, nationality, and race, which were hotly contested in local and state politics.

3. Politics and reform are brought together not only in cities but also in the Populist revolt and the election of 1896, which marked the 1890s as a "pivotal" turning point in American attitudes and political party alignments.

(3) LEARNING GOALS

Familiarity with Basic Knowledge

After reading this chapter, you should be able to:

1. Characterize Gilded Age politicians, party campaigns, and the two political parties, and briefly explain the three major national and three typical local political issues of the late nineteenth century.

2. Define the following terms: Gospel of Wealth, social Darwinism, reform Darwinism, pragmatism, Social Gospel, Gilded Age.

3. Describe the purpose and the programs of the settlement house movement, the Social Gospel, and urban reformers.

4. State and briefly explain the results of two or three areas of legislation Congress considered in 1890, and explain the causes of the depression of 1893 - 1897.

5. Explain the party strategies, campaign issues, and results of the election of 1896.

Practice in Historical Thinking Skills

After reading this chapter, you should be able to:

1. Analyze the relationship between national and local politics in the Gilded Age and the middle-class movement for reform.

2. Explain the motivations and programs of urban reformers, the Social Gospel and settlement workers, and those seeking women's suffrage.

3. Analyze the significance of the election of 1896 as a response to the crises of the pivotal 1890s.

(4) IMPORTANT DATES AND NAMES TO KNOW

1873	Congress demonetizes silver
1875	Specie Resumption Act
1877	Rutherford B. Hayes becomes president
1878	Bland-Allison Act
1879	Henry George, *Progress and Poverty*
1880	James A. Garfield elected president
1881	Garfield assassinated; Chester A. Arthur succeeds to presidency
1883	Pendleton Civil Service Act
1884	Grover Cleveland elected president W. D. Howells, *The Rise of Silas Lapham*
1887	College Settlement House Association founded
1888	Edward Bellamy, *Looking Backward* Benjamin Harrison elected president
1889	Jane Addams establishes Hull House Andrew Carnegie promulgates the "Gospel of Wealth"
1890	General Federation of Women's Clubs founded Sherman Anti-Trust Act Sherman Silver Purchase Act McKinley Tariff Election bill defeated
1890s	Wyoming, Colorado, Utah, and Idaho grant woman suffrage
1892	Cleveland elected president for the second time

Populist party wins over one million votes
Homestead Steel strike

1893   World's Columbian Exposition in Chicago

1893 - 1897   Financial panic and depression

1894   Pullman strike
Coxey's march on Washington

1895   *United States* v. *E. C. Knight*

1896   Charles Sheldon, *In His Steps*
Populist party fuses with Democrats
William McKinley elected president

1897   "Golden Rule" Jones elected mayor of Toledo, Ohio
Economic recovery begins

Other Names to Know

James G. Blaine	Roscoe Conkling
Jane Addams	Vida Scudder
Francis Willard	John Dewey
Kate Chopin	Charlotte Perkins Gilman
Horatio Alger	Andrew Carnegie
Herbert Spencer	William Graham Sumner
Dwight Moody	William Jennings Bryan
Charles Eliot	Walter Rauschenbusch
Washington Gladden	William James

(5) GLOSSARY OF IMPORTANT TERMS

Gilded Age: term coined by Mark Twain and C. D. Warner referring to the late-nineteenth-century preoccupation with making money, also suggesting superficiality and corruption

Gospel of Wealth: the doctrine, identified with Andrew Carnegie, that the rich had a responsibility, a stewardship, to use their wealth for the public good

social Darwinism: the application of Darwin's theories of the struggle for existence and natural selection (survival of the fittest) in the biological world to the human world of socioeconomic affairs: the strong succeed while the weak do not and should not

Social Gospel: movement in churches to apply Christian principles to social concerns, especially in cities and factories

suffragists: women actively working for the right to vote (not *suffragettes*—a diminutive, often insulting term)

bossism: system of urban government in which the local party chief, or boss, dispenses many favors and engages in various forms of corruption in return for votes and financial support

pragmatism: an American philosophy that finds the best test of truth in consequences, in how well an idea works

laissez-faire: a doctrine that argued that all would benefit from an economic life free from government interference

(6) ENRICHMENT IDEAS

1. Material culture can provide insights in recovering the social and political life of the past. The study of material artifacts generated by the campaign of 1896 reveals much about the values and issues of American political life. Mail-order catalogs, which show dress styles and the goods purchased by Americans in a given age, can also reveal much about a culture. Today's households are usually inundated with catalogs. Compare a catalog from the Gilded Age with some of the catalogs you receive. What similarities and differences in middle-class life and consumption patterns are suggested? What do you conclude about leisure and gender roles? What do the buttons, bumper stickers, and material artifacts of a recent political campaign show about contemporary political behavior?

2. To what extent do middle-class men and women play a role in local, state, or national politics today? Identify and interview some persons active in politics. Find out what their concerns are, why they are active, and how effective they think they are. Then compare them to the middle-class reformers of the 1890s.

3. The excitement of the Democratic party convention in 1896 and Bryan's "Cross of Gold" speech is worth special research and attention. So is the election itself. Whose side would you have been on? Why?

(7) SAMPLE TEST AND EXAMINATION QUESTIONS

Multiple choice: Choose the best answer.

1. *Looking Backward* was a utopian novel written by
   a. Henry Adams
   b. Henry George
   c. Edward Bellamy
   d. Kate Chopin

2. Political parties in the late nineteenth century were concerned primarily with
   a. patronage
   b. ideological consistency
   c. racial issues
   d. foreign affairs

3. Tariffs in the late nineteenth century were
   a. extremely high and protective
   b. subject to individual adjustments by the president
   c. basically high, although usually a mixture of high and low rates
   d. tied to coinage each time they came before Congress

4. Supporters of hard money wanted
   a. to increase the supply of paper money
   b. to increase the supply of silver
   c. to make greenbacks convertible to specie
   d. to encourage inflation

5. During the Gilded Age,
   a. the Democrats were ascendant
   b. the Republicans dominated
   c. third parties disrupted the political process
   d. the two major parties were evenly matched

6. Before 1888 political parties were financed by
   a. taxes
   b. a percentage of salaries of patronage workers
   c. corporations
   d. political action committees

7. The large turnout of voters in state and local elections in the Gilded Age meant that voters were probably concerned with
   a. getting jobs and favors as a result of their vote
   b. ethnocultural issues like immigration, temperance, and parochial schools
   c. specific local issues like race and railroad rates
   d. all of the above

8. According to the "Gospel of Wealth,"
   a. the rich had an obligation to become ministers
   b. the rich had an obligation to use their money to help others
   c. Americans were becoming more democratic
   d. profits should be reinvested for more profits

9. All of the following are identified with social Darwinism EXCEPT
   a. Herbert Spencer
   b. William Graham Sumner
   c. Henry Adams
   d. Andrew Carnegie

10. The settlement house movement
    a. blended idealism and practical goals
    b. typified the utter unreality of middle-class women
    c. was at odds with sociology
    d. was a hotbed of socialism

11. Urban bosses
    a. taxed their constituents
    b. offered "welfare" support to people who voted for them
    c. mostly ran saloons
    d. were a figment of reformers' imagination

12. The younger generation of women suffragists in the 1890s primarily
    a. used expedient arguments
    b. cited principles
    c. marched on Washington
    d. quoted Saint Paul

13. During the depression of 1893 - 1897, what portion of the American labor force was unemployed?
    a. a half
    b. a third
    c. a fifth
    d. a tenth

14. The election of 1896 was significant because
    a. the Democrats became the party of prosperity and national greatness
    b. the Republicans became the dominant party in the United States
    c. the Populists became a permanently significant force in American politics
    d. all of the above

15. Can you put the Gilded Age presidents in the right order?
    a. Hayes, Garfield, Arthur, Cleveland, Harrison
    b. Hayes, Grant, Cleveland, Garfield, Cleveland
    c. Grant, Garfield, Arthur, Harrison, Cleveland
    d. Garfield, Arthur, Hayes, Cleveland, Grant

Essays

1. Explain why the 1890s was a "pivotal" decade.

2. Bossism was a national political response to urban life and shifting social patterns. Discuss with evidence.

3. Middle-class reformers in the Gilded Age were concerned with modifying the political and social system, not discarding it. Discuss.

4. Analyze the significance of the election of 1896 for American politics.

THE BICYCLE

At the Centennial Exhibition in Philadelphia in 1876, a Boston merchant, Albert A. Pope, was so intrigued by the display of an English high-wheeled bicycle that he went to England to study its manufacture. Two years later, "the father of the bicycle in America" began making a domestic version, called the Columbia, in Hartford, Connecticut. In 1887, the Pope Manufacturing Company shifted its production to the even more popular "safety" bicycle, a chain-driven model with two wheels of equal size very much like those we ride today. Within a decade, more than 300 companies were producing over a million bicycles a year, and millions of Americans, mostly middle-class, were finding a new mobility and freedom.

The bicycle craze peaked in 1896 and 1897, but the importance of this innovation in transportation was far-reaching, for it heralded several major technological and marketing developments of the twentieth century. As Joseph Woodworth wrote in *American Tool Making and Interchangeable Manufacturing* in 1907, "The manufacture of the bicycle . . . brought out the capabilities of the American mechanic as nothing else had ever done. It demonstrated to the world that he and his kind were capable of designing and making special machinery, tools, fixtures, and devices for economic manufacturing in a manner truly marvelous." Moreover, Woodworth went on, the bicycle led to the "installation of the interchangeable system of manufacture in a thousand and one shops where it was formerly thought to be impractical."

It is revealing that Pope began his manufacture of bicycles in a Hartford sewing machine company, which itself had started as a rifle plant, for the manufacturing techniques were virtually identical for all three products. Following the established New England armory principles of machine-produced interchangeable parts, bicycle parts were drop-forged and then machine-tooled and finished. In a noteworthy innovation, again heralding twentieth-century techniques, a Chicago firm, the Western Wheel Works, developed presses for stamping out parts from large sheets of steel. This technique was superior to drop-forging because it was more precise and required less machine tooling.

In an *Atlantic Monthly* article published in 1898, W. J. McGee, reviewing 50 years of developments in modern science, suggested that the bicycle was a typical American invention because it not only stimulated inventiveness and new production techniques but also "developed individuality, judgement, and prompt decision on the part of its users." Even more important, McGee wrote, "the bicycle has broken the pernicious differential of the sexes" by making available a model for women that opened up areas of freedom, mobility, and sport previously unknown. The bicycle even changed "the bonds of fashion," McGee said, and was "daily impressing Spartan strength and grace, and more than Spartan intelligence, on the mothers of coming generations."

One of McGee's insights was that the bicycle was shaping national character by "transforming itself and its rider into a single thing," thus providing autonomy of movement and prefiguring the development of the automobile. In 1895, Albert Pope predicted "the advent of the motor-carriage" and employed Hiram Percy Maxim to begin building experimental automobiles. As Maxim put it later, the bicycle "created a new demand which it was beyond the ability of the railroad to supply. Then it came about that the bicycle could not satisfy the demand which it had created. A mechanically propelled vehicle was wanted instead of a foot-propelled one, and we now know that the automobile was the answer." With the principles and practice of mass production, interchangeable parts, sheet metal presswork, and democratic use already established, the bicycle almost literally "paved the road" for Henry Ford.

20

Becoming a World Power

(1) CHAPTER OUTLINE

As the United States Senate debates whether to annex the Philippine Islands, tension mounts near Manila as Filipinos and Americans confront each other across an uneasy neutral zone. While on patrol, Private William Grayson encounters some Filipino soldiers and kills them, and general hostilities break out. The result is a nasty three-year war of suppression, marking a crucial change in America's role in the world.

Steps Toward Empire
America as a Model Society
Early Expansionism
Expansion After Seward

Expansionism in the 1890s
Profits: Searching for Overseas Markets
Patriotism: Asserting National Power
Piety: The Missionary Impulse
Politics: Manipulating Public Opinion

Cuba and the Philippines
The Road to War
"A Splendid Little War"
The Philippines Debates and War
Expansionism Triumphant

Roosevelt's Energetic Diplomacy
Foreign Policy as Darwinian Struggle
Taking the Panama Canal
Policeman of the Caribbean
Opening the Door to China
Japan and the Balance of Power
Preventing War in Europe

Conclusion: The Responsibilities of Power

(2) SIGNIFICANT THEMES AND HIGHLIGHTS

1. The opening anecdote highlights the American annexation of the Philippines by the Senate and the three-year war suppressing the revolt that followed. This episode reflects the major motivations, policies, and problems of American expansionism in the period from 1890 to 1912, the focus of this chapter.

2. The Philippine experience and the wider expressions of expansionism during this period reflect and reveal fundamental and enduring dilemmas of America's relationship with the rest of the world. These ripples start as far back as the Puritans and flow forward to familiar patterns of foreign affairs in our own time.

3. Historical analogies are dangerous, and one must be cautious in making them. Human situations and international relations are never exactly the same. Nevertheless, many are similar enough to be instructive. This chapter can be read, therefore, to understand not only the foreign policy events between 1890 and 1912 but also those in America's recent past and, indeed, those reported in today's newspapers.

4. Although some effort has been made to reflect the common soldier's war experiences, ordinary people play less of a role in this chapter than in others. At the center is an era in foreign affairs in which the United States became a world power. Leading the way was Theodore Roosevelt, a most uncommon person.

(3) LEARNING GOALS

Familiarity with Basic Knowledge

After reading this chapter, you should be able to:

1. Identify two or three major foreign policy pronouncements that influenced nineteenth-century American policies.

2. Explain each of the four major motivations for American expansionism in the 1890s.

3. Describe the series of events that led to the Spanish-American War and those that led to the annexation of and war with the Philippines.

4. State several arguments for and against the annexation of the Philippines.

5. Locate each of the following on a map and state why it is important.

Cuba	Puerto Rico	Manila
Panama Canal	Hong Kong	Santo Domingo
Guam	Philippine Islands	(Dominican Republic)
Portsmouth, New Hampshire	Manchuria	Morocco

Hawaiian Islands   Samoan Islands   Venezuela

6. Explain the principles of Theodore Roosevelt's foreign policy and describe the role of the United States in Asia, Europe, and the Caribbean between 1890 and 1912.

Practice in Historical Thinking Skills

After reading this chapter, you should be able to:

1. Compare and contrast American involvement with the Cubans and with the Filipinos, and develop your own position either supporting or rejecting the annexation of the Philippines.

2. Assess the effectiveness of Roosevelt's foreign policy.

3. Evaluate the extent to which the United States continues to experience dilemmas in its international relationships.

(4) IMPORTANT DATES AND NAMES TO KNOW

1823	Monroe Doctrine
1857	Trade opens with Japan
1867	Alaska purchased from Russia
1870	Failure to annex Santo Domingo (Dominican Republic)
1875	Sugar reciprocity treaty with Hawaii
1877	United States acquires naval base at Pearl Harbor
1878	United States acquires naval station in Samoa
1882	Chinese Exclusion Act
1889	First Pan-American conference
1890	Alfred Mahan, *Influence of Sea Power upon History*
1893	Hawaiian coup by American sugar growers
1895	Cuban revolt against Spanish Venezuelan boundary dispute

| 1896 | Weyler's reconcentration policy in Cuba |
| | McKinley-Bryan presidential campaign |

| 1897 | Theodore Roosevelt's speech to Naval War College |

1898	Jan.	De Lôme letter
	Feb.	Sinking of the battleship *Maine*
	April	Spanish-American War begins; Teller Amendment
	May	Dewey takes Manila Bay
	July	Annexation of Hawaiian Islands
	Aug.	Americans liberate Manila; war ends
	Dec.	Treaty of Paris; annexation of Philippines

1899	Filipino-American War begins
	Senate ratifies Treaty of Paris
	Acquisition of American Samoa

| 1899 - 1900 | Open Door notes |

| 1900 | Boxer Rebellion in China |
| | McKinley reelected |

| 1901 | Supreme Court insular cases |
| | McKinley assassinated; Theodore Roosevelt becomes president |

1902	Filipino-American War ends
	U.S. military occupation of Cuba ends
	Platt Amendment
	Venezuelan debt crisis

| 1903 | Panamanian revolt and independence |
| | Hay - Bunau - Varilla Treaty |

| 1904 | Roosevelt Corollary |

| 1904 - 1905 | Russo-Japanese War ended by treaty signed in Portsmouth, NH |

| 1904 - 1906 | United States intervenes in Nicaragua, Guatemala, and Cuba |

| 1905 - 1906 | Moroccan crisis |

| 1906 | Theodore Roosevelt receives Nobel Peace Prize |

| 1907 | Gentleman's agreement with Japan |

1908	Root-Takahira Agreement
1909	U.S. Navy ("Great White Fleet") sails around the world
1911	United States intervenes in Nicaragua
1914	Panama Canal opens World War I begins
1916	Partial home rule granted to the Philippines

Other Names to Know

Emilio Aguinaldo	John Hay
Richard Olney	Philippe Bunau-Varilla
George F. Hoar	William Seward
Ernest H. Crosby	Henry Cabot Lodge
Josiah Strong	Alfred Thayer Mahan
Kaiser Wilhelm II	George Dewey

(5) GLOSSARY OF IMPORTANT TERMS

"white man's burden": idea of the special responsibility of "civilized" nations like England and the United States to uplift and care for "uncivilized" nations, as popularized in a poem by Rudyard Kipling

missionary diplomacy: the belief that American ideas and ideals, especially representative government and Protestantism, should be spread around the world

anti-imperialists: people opposing American expansionism in 1898 and 1899

Roosevelt Corollary to the Monroe Doctrine: established the primary right of the United States to intervene in Latin America to maintain stability and order

dollar diplomacy: foreign policy featuring an increase in U.S. trade and investments in other countries, thus enabling the United States to influence affairs in those countries

(6) ENRICHMENT IDEAS

1. As suggested by Recovering The Past, find other political cartoons about Teddy Roosevelt and American foreign policy during this period (or about other subjects: Bryan, McKinley, and the election of 1900), and analyze how they make their editorial point.

2. On a map of the continental United States, fill in the various parts of the expanding territory of the United States from 1783 to 1853, indicating how each new section was acquired. On a map of the world, locate and fill in all U.S. acquisitions (and interventions) around the world from the Civil War to World War I. What obvious conclusions do you draw?

3. Consider the extent to which the United States still tries to do good in an imperfect world and seeks to be both powerful and loved. Is the United States today basically isolationist or internationalist? To what extent is America still a model for the rest of the world?

4. Historical analogies: The Greek historian Thucydides, writing 2,400 years ago, said that, human nature being what it is, "events which happened in the past . . . will, at some time or other and in much the same ways, be repeated in the future." Despite the wisdom of one of the earliest and greatest historians, historical analogies are dangerous, and one must be cautious in making them. Human situations and international relations, though similar, are never exactly the same.

Nevertheless, many Americans have drawn an analogy between the war against Aguinaldo's rebels following the annexation of the Philippines and the war in Vietnam in the 1960s and early 1970s. Many have continued the analogy to the U.S. relationship with and role in Central America in the 1980s and 1990s. What do you think of these historical analogies? Is it helpful to make them or not? Is American foreign policy well served by comparing the Central American situation to Vietnam or to the Philippines? What are the dangers of making historical analogies?

Consider other historical analogies and the extent to which they inform and enhance understanding or mislead and lead to dangerous decisions. Examples: Secretary of State Dean Rusk's frequent comparison of a weak policy toward North Vietnam in the mid-1960s with England's appeasement policy toward Nazi Germany in the 1930s, or the argument of people who oppose increased nuclear weapons because earlier arms races in history, like that between Germany and England before World War I, always led to war. The Persian Gulf War—Saddam Hussein and Hitler? What others can you think of?

(7) SAMPLE TEST AND EXAMINATION QUESTIONS

Multiple choice: Choose the best answer.

1. In the early summer of 1898, the Filipino rebels under Aguinaldo
   a. looked forward to American help in winning their independence from Spain
   b. were fighting minor skirmishes against both the Americans and the Spanish
   c. liberated Manila and declared their independence, with the warm support of American officials
   d. were languishing in Spanish jails waiting for Dewey's rescue

2. The war in the Philippines marked the first time
    a. Americans had fought a guerilla war
    b. draftees made up much of the army
    c. American soldiers fought outside North America
    d. American troops were under foreign command

3. Compared to the Spanish-American War, the battle casualties and costs of the American-Philippine War were
    a. about the same
    b. much lower
    c. much higher
    d. unknown because of so much disease

4. The "city on the hill" refers to
    a. America's mission as a model society for the world
    b. Sodom and Gomorrah as examples of the sinfulness of man
    c. San Francisco's image to Japanese immigrants
    d. Jerusalem and the Hebrew idea of a chosen people

5. The United States acquired all of the following prior to 1898 EXCEPT
    a. the Midway Islands
    b. Pearl Harbor
    c. Alaska
    d. the Panama Canal Zone

6. As a result of the Treaty of Paris, the United States acquired all of the following EXCEPT
    a. Guam
    b. Puerto Rico
    c. Cuba
    d. the Philippines

7. According to the missionary ideal,
    a. western political institutions were superior to any others
    b. Protestantism was better than Catholicism
    c. Western values should be spread all over the world
    d. all of the above

8. The battleship *Maine* was sunk by
    a. Cuban rebels
    b. Spanish sailors
    c. U.S. Navy Seals in disguise
    d. a still unknown cause, but probably an overheated boiler

9. The Spanish-American War began for all of the following reasons EXCEPT
   a. the persistence of the Cuban rebels
   b. the Spanish government's erratic, confusing policies
   c. McKinley's determination to liberate and uplift the Cuban people
   d. the influence of the sensationalist press on the American conscience

10. The anti-imperialists opposed the annexation of the Philippines
    a. exclusively for idealistic, humane reasons
    b. mainly for fear of assimilation with brown-skinned people
    c. for a mixture of idealistic, base, and practical reasons
    d. largely because higher taxes would result in big government and a loss of freedom

11. Roosevelt
    a. saw the world as one divided between uncivilized and civilized nations
    b. thought that the civilized nations would have to battle it out to see who would control the uncivilized world
    c. preferred starting wars to settling them
    d. spoke loudly and carried a big stick

12. The Roosevelt Corollary
    a. justified the U.S. role as policeman of the Caribbean
    b. justified U.S. intervention in European affairs
    c. warned Russia out of Manchuria
    d. all of the above

13. Which of the following best describes American trade with China?
    a. Although slow to develop, after Hay's Open Door notes, trade skyrocketed.
    b. Trade jumped from one percent of all U.S. trade in 1870 to more than 20 percent by 1910.
    c. Although there were increases, the China trade was less in reality than in theory.
    d. After reaching a peak of 12 percent in 1899, the China trade decreased as a result of the Boxer Rebellion.

14. Roosevelt
    a. had little respect for China
    b. had little respect for Japan
    c. initially wanted Japan to counterbalance the growing power of Russia
    d. wanted Russia, as a great power, to police the Far East

15. American foreign policy under Roosevelt can be characterized by all of the following EXCEPT
    a. a desire to prevent European war
    b. friendship with Great Britain
    c. personal diplomacy
    d. indifference toward Germany

Identify and show a relationship between each of the following pairs:

Josiah Strong	*and*	Henry Cabot Lodge
Portsmouth, New Hampshire	*and*	Algeciras, Spain
Morocco	*and*	Manchuria
Guantanamo	*and*	Pearl Harbor
dollar diplomacy	*and*	missionary diplomacy
New Panama Company	*and*	Clayton-Bulwer Treaty
"Great White Fleet"	*and*	Chinese Exclusion

Essays

1. Discuss the relationship between and ironies involved in the Spanish-American and the Philippine-American Wars.

2. Discuss the extent to which United States foreign policy still faces a dilemma of doing good in an imperfect world, of being both powerful and loved. Analyze the roots, major manifestations, and enduring nature of this dilemma.

3. The United States learned about the costs of formal empire in the Philippines but did not give up its imperial ambitions, as its policy toward Latin America reveals. Discuss with specific evidence.

4. American foreign policy in this period was evidence of the agricultural and industrial transformation after the Civil War. Discuss. (You may need to review Chapters 17 and 18 before writing this essay.)

Identify and Interpret: Quotation
(that is, state who, what, where, when, and why significant)

It is not true that the United States feels any land hunger or entertains any projects as regards the other nations of the Western Hemisphere save such as are for their welfare. All that this country desires is to see the neighboring countries stable, orderly, and prosperous. Any country whose people conduct themselves well can count upon our hearty friendship. If a nation shows that it knows how to act with reasonable efficiency and decency in social and political matters, if it keeps order and pays its obligations, it need fear no interference from the United States. Chronic wrongdoing, or an impotence which results in a general loosening of the ties of civilized society, may in America, as elsewhere, ultimately require intervention by some civilized nation, and in the Western Hemisphere the adherence of the United States to the Monroe Doctrine may lead the United States, however reluctantly, in flagrant cases of such wrongdoing or impotence, to the exercise of an international police power.

Map Question

Locate the following on the accompanying map.

1. Philippine Islands
2. Manila
3. Hawaiian Islands
4. Korea
5. Panama Canal
6. Santo Domingo
7. Venezuela
8. Portsmouth, New Hampshire
9. Manchuria
10. Guam
11. Samoan Islands
12. Cuba
13. Puerto Rico
14. Nicaragua
15. Alaska
16. Japan

A MODERNIZING PEOPLE
1900 - 1945

The first half of the twentieth century was filled with tumultuous changes. Two destructive and tragic world wars and the worst economic depression the modern world has endured had lasting impact on all Americans. But so did the spectacular advances in technology. In 1900, the United States was still a predominantly rural nation depending for transportation on the railroad and the horse. By 1945, the automobile, the airplane, plastics, radio, television, and the atomic bomb had transformed the country, and electricity and the telephone had become commonplace in a nation where the majority of Americans lived in urban areas.

Chapter 21, "The Progressives Confront Industrial Capitalism," discusses progressivism, the first modern American reform movement. It examines the nation's struggle to maintain democratic order in an urban and industrial age and to adapt its institutions to the arrival of millions of immigrants. The middle-class reformers who thought they knew what was best for these immigrants, and for the other migrants to American cities, sometimes overlooked individual liberties as they sought to promote justice for the many.

Chapter 22, "The Great War," describes U.S. involvement in World War I, a conflict most Americans initially wanted to avoid. But once committed, the United States turned the war into a crusade to "make the world safe for democracy," in Woodrow Wilson's words. Yet government authorities often arrested and jailed people who spoke out against the war. The wartime situation also had a tremendous economic impact. It gave new opportunities to blacks and other minorities and began the process of government-business cooperation that would increase bureaucracy and change the very nature of the American system of free enterprise.

Chapter 23, "Affluence and Anxiety," covers the period between World War I and the stock market crash of 1929—a time of prosperity, technological change, and business expansion. The chapter also tells the story of those left out of the prosperity of the 1920s and shows how the decade was marked by fear, intolerance, and the Red Scare.

Chapter 24, "The Great Depression and the New Deal," focuses on the Depression decade, a time of unprecedented economic collapse that threatened the very survival of American democracy and American capitalism. It also discusses the New Deal, a major American reform movement that promoted the power of the federal government to stimulate the economy and to pass a variety of social programs. Although the New Deal introduced key elements of the modern welfare state and greatly increased the regulatory power of the federal government, it never proved able to lift the country from economic depression. Moreover, the increasing power of the government raised the question of how individual liberty could be preserved under centralized governmental authority.

In Chapter 25, "World War II," we discover that war, rather than the New Deal, ended the Depression. World War II stimulated the economy and at the same time released American crusading zeal in an all-out effort to defeat Germany and Japan. The war meant opportunity for many as it meant death and despair for others. During the war, Americans tended to see the world divided between good and evil; yet the United States emerged as the most prosperous and most powerful nation on earth. The euphoria would not last long as peace devolved into the Cold War and competition with the Soviet Union for world domination.

21

The Progressives Confront Industrial Capitalism

(1) CHAPTER OUTLINE

A young midwestern lawyer, Frances Kellor, trains herself as a social reformer because she believes in the progressive faith that moral vision and efficient expertise can eliminate poverty and inequality. As the first woman appointed to head a state agency, she is one of the leaders of the effort to foster both social justice and middle-class values for immigrant workers in America.

The Social Justice Movement
  The Progressive World View
  The Muckrakers
  Working Women and Children
  Home and School
  Crusades Against Saloons, Brothels, and Movie Houses

The Worker in the Progressive Era
  Adjusting to Industrial Labor
  Union Organizing
  Garment Workers and the Triangle Fire
  Radical Labor

Reform in the Cities and States
  Municipal Reformers
  City Beautiful
  Reform in the States

Theodore Roosevelt and the Square Deal
  A Strong and Controversial President
  Dealing with the Trusts
  Meat Inspection and Pure Food and Drugs
  Conservation Versus Preservation
  Progressivism for Whites Only
  William Howard Taft
  The Election of 1912

Woodrow Wilson and the New Freedom
   Tariff and Banking Reform
   Moving Closer to a New Nationalism

Conclusion: The Limits of Progressivism

(2) SIGNIFICANT THEMES AND HIGHLIGHTS

1. The work of Frances Kellor reflects the twin goals of urban professional reformers in their response to industrialism, immigration, and urbanism. They sought to achieve social justice and reform as well as order and efficiency. Their faith in social research and expert commissions to solve social problems was nearly as strong as their optimism that they would succeed in cleaning up America.

2. Kellor's life also reveals the progressives' ambiguous attitude toward the poor immigrant workers they sought to help. Progressive reformers were well intentioned and sincere in their desire to alleviate social misery and expand opportunity at the same time as they were paternalistic, elitist, and racist in their effort to make immigrants into good Americanized citizens with middle-class values.

3. In this chapter, the work of progressive reformers is shown at the three political levels of American society—cities, states, and the national government—where the differences between the New Nationalism of Theodore Roosevelt and the New Freedom of Woodrow Wilson are described.

4. Throughout the chapter, note the important role of women in progressive reform and the underlying tone of moral concern and family values that permeated the movement.

(3) LEARNING GOALS

Familiarity with Basic Knowledge

After reading this chapter, you should be able to:

1. Enumerate and briefly describe several reform goals of the progressives and their views on child labor, working women, education, and vice.

2. Outline the differing goals and programs for factory reform held by working-class leaders and by progressives.

3. List and briefly describe the major goals and programs of municipal reformers and progressive reformers at the state level.

4. Describe Theodore Roosevelt's attitudes toward and programs for trusts, conservation, and blacks and show how they differed from those of William Howard Taft.

5. Describe the Progressive party and its programs.

6. State the major pieces of progressive legislation passed during the presidency of Woodrow Wilson.

Practice in Historical Thinking Skills

After reading this chapter, you should be able to:

1. Explain the tension among progressives between their twin goals of achieving social justice reform on the one hand and order and efficiency on the other.

2. Compare and contrast the political philosophy of Roosevelt's New Nationalism and Wilson's New Freedom.

3. Assess the success of the progressive movement by analyzing its achievements and limitations.

(4) IMPORTANT DATES AND NAMES TO KNOW

1901	McKinley assassinated; Theodore Roosevelt becomes president
	Robert La Follette elected governor of Wisconsin
	Tom Johnson elected mayor of Cleveland
	Model tenement house bill passed in New York
	Formation of U.S. Steel
1902	Anthracite coal strike
1903	Women's Trade Union League founded
	Elkins Act
1904	Roosevelt reelected
	Lincoln Steffens, *The Shame of the Cities*
1905	Frederic C. Howe, *The City: The Hope of Democracy*
	Industrial Workers of the World (IWW) formed
1906	Upton Sinclair, *The Jungle*
	Hepburn Act
	Meat Inspection Act
	Pure Food and Drug Act

1907	Financial panic
1908	*Muller* v. *Oregon* *Danbury Hatters* case William H. Taft elected president
1909	Herbert Croly, *The Promise of American Life* National Association for the Advancement of Colored People (NAACP) founded
1910	Ballinger-Pinchot controversy Mann Act
1911	Frederick Taylor publishes *The Principles of Scientific Management* Triangle Shirtwaist Company fire
1912	Woodrow Wilson elected president Progressive party founded by Theodore Roosevelt Children's Bureau established in Department of Labor Industrial Relations Commission founded
1913	Sixteenth Amendment (income tax) ratified Underwood Tariff Federal Reserve System established Seventeenth Amendment (direct election of senators) passed
1914	Clayton Act Federal Trade Commission Act American Federation of Labor (AFL) has over 2 million members Ludlow (Colorado) Massacre

Other Names to Know

Ida Tarbell	Frederick Taylor
Florence Kelley	Eugene Debs
Jane Addams	Charlotte Perkins Gilman
Josephine Goldmark	Gifford Pinchot
Louis Brandeis	W. E. B. Du Bois
Jacob Riis	William English Walling
Lawrence Veiller	"Mother" Jones
John Dewey	"Big Bill" Haywood

(5) GLOSSARY OF IMPORTANT TERMS

muckrakers: journalists and other writers in the first decade of the twentieth century who exposed various social and political problems in urban industrial American life

social justice: issues of concern to progressive reformers, such as child labor, working women, juvenile justice, tenement house reform, education, saloons, movie houses, and prostitution ("the social evil")

scientific management: theory of factory management based on Frederick Taylor's time-efficiency studies aimed at making workers maximally efficient

City Beautiful movement: effort by progressives to bring parks, playgrounds, grand buildings and boulevards, and other forms of culture to cities in order to make them both more beautiful and more livable

Niagara movement: growing out of a 1905 conference in Niagara Falls, Canada, called by W. E. B. Du Bois, a movement of young black intellectuals calling for "persistent manly agitation" in achieving equal political, civil, and economic rights

New Nationalism: Roosevelt's program in 1912 for increasing the power of the federal government to regulate business and industry and to achieve social justice and equal rights for labor, women, children, and other groups

New Freedom: Wilson's program in 1912 for reducing central power in order to restore older forms of economic competition and equality of opportunity

conservation: planned protection of the nation's resources so they will be available for the use of the people for activities like logging, grazing, and energy production

preservation: protect the land in a wilderness state; advocated by John Muir

(6) ENRICHMENT IDEAS

1. Using the examples in the textbook or a larger collection of photographs of urban slums, street children, and immigrant workers by Jacob Riis and Lewis Hine, analyze the photographs and discuss the questions in Recovering The Past dealing with the use of the documentary photograph for purposes of reform.

2. Make a chart showing the similarities and differences between the political ideals, policies, and programs of Theodore Roosevelt and those of Woodrow Wilson.

(7) SAMPLE TEST AND EXAMINATION QUESTIONS

Multiple choice: Choose the best answer.

1. Progressive movement goals included all of the following EXCEPT
   a. playgrounds and parks
   b. free silver
   c. regulated trusts
   d. prohibition

2. The muckrakers were primarily concerned with
   a. urban graft and corruption
   b. Standard Oil and other corporations
   c. poverty
   d. all of the above

3. The social justice movement sought to do all of the following EXCEPT
   a. improve housing
   b. abolish child labor
   c. improve schools
   d. achieve racial equality

4. According to progressive reformers, women workers
   a. should have the right to work as many hours as men
   b. deserved protective legislation because they were weaker than men
   c. should stay at home and have babies instead of work
   d. should supervise children better in factories

5. Progressive educators
   a. imitated European forms of education
   b. taught immigrants in their own languages
   c. were child-centered rather than subject-centered
   d. none of the above

6. In talking about "the social evil," reformers referred to
   a. saloons
   b. movie houses
   c. racism
   d. prostitution

7. The AFL
   a. strongly supported Taylorism
   b. encouraged the organization of women workers
   c. condemned socialism
   d. sought a merger with the IWW

8. All of the following were radical labor leaders EXCEPT
   a. Eugene Debs
   b. William Jennings Bryan
   c. "Big Bill" Haywood
   d. Daniel De Leon

9. The commission form of city government was first developed in
   a. Boston
   b. Dayton
   c. Galveston
   d. Chicago

10. Progressives at the state level passed laws
    a. providing social justice measures for farmers
    b. granting women the right to vote
    c. creating commissions to try to check the power of special-interest groups
    d. regulating interstate commerce

11. President Roosevelt's approach to trusts was
    a. to support bigness while opposing misconduct
    b. to urge stronger antitrust legislation
    c. to restore freedom of competition by vigorous trustbusting
    d. to encourage monopoly control of railroads

12. Roosevelt's attitude toward blacks was illustrated most clearly by
    a. his insensitive handling of black soldiers in the Brownsville, Texas, incident
    b. his vigorous enforcement of the Fourteenth Amendment
    c. his warm friendship with Booker T. Washington
    d. his support for W. E. B. Du Bois's Niagara movement

13. Woodrow Wilson won the presidency in 1912 primarily because
    a. the American people were tired of progressivism
    b. political dominance had shifted back to the Democratic party
    c. Roosevelt's Progressive party split the Republican vote
    d. the threat of war in Europe made Wilson an attractive alternative to Roosevelt's military bluster

14. All of the following pieces of progressive legislation were passed under Wilson EXCEPT
    a. the Mann-Elkins Act
    b. the Underwood Tariff
    c. the Federal Reserve system
    d. the Clayton Anti-Trust Act

15.   According to the chapter author, progressive regulatory laws
       a.   succeeded in checking the growing power of trusts
       b.   worked better with the oil and tobacco industries than with railroads
       c.   tended to strengthen corporate capitalism rather than to weaken it
       d.   should have been enforced more against unions than corporations

Identify and show a relationship between each of the following pairs.

Frederick Taylor	*and*	Samuel Gompers
Jacob Riis	*and*	Lawrence Veiller
Robert La Follette	*and*	Tom Johnson
The Jungle	*and*	the Meat Inspection Act
John Dewey	*and*	Florence Kelley
"Mother" Jones	*and*	the Ludlow Massacre
Eugene Debs	*and*	William H. Taft
Muller v. *Oregon*	*and*	Triangle fire

Essays

1. Compare and contrast the presidential administrations of Roosevelt, Taft, and Wilson, indicating which one succeeded most in fulfilling progressive goals and why you think so.

2. Describe a "typical" progressive, and explain why concern for child labor and working women were "typical" progressive causes.

3. Explain the tension among progressives between their twin goals of social justice on the one hand and order and efficiency on the other. In which area do you think they were most successful in achieving concrete changes? Support your answer with specific examples.

4. Discuss the role of women in the progressive movement.

Identify and Interpret: Chart

(that is, first, study the chart and describe what it shows; second, analyze the chart by explaining some of the reasons behind the patterns you see; third, assess the larger significance of the chart)

	# of addresses	# of families	Children Boys	Girls	Unmarried Men	Women	Predominating Nationalities
Census of One Hundred and Twenty-nine Tenements Where Disorderly Conditions Prevailed—January, February, March, April 1909							
South of 14th Street & East of Broadway	50	847	525	563	242	78	Russian, Polish, Rumanian, Austrian, Jewish, Italian, Bohemian, Hungarian, German, Cuban, Irish, Galician, American
West 104th Street to West 153d Street	28	340	49	71	13	15	French, Norwegian, Danish, German, Irish, Swedish, Jewish, Portuguese, West Indian, American
East 79th Street to 124th Street	16	173	122	132	63	37	Colored and White Americans, Irish, Italian, German, Russian, Rumanian, Swedish, West Indian
Bronx	2	28	9	11	6	4	Jewish, German, Irish, American, Italian
Brooklyn	33	133	94	83	47	22	Irish, Italian, German, Greek, Swedish, Russian, Scotch, Polish, Norwegian, Colored and White Americans
TOTAL	129	1,521	799	860	371	156	

Source: *The Social Evil in New York City: A Study of Law Enforcement by The Research Committee of the Committee of Fourteen* (New York: Andrew H. Kellogg Co., 1910), p. 223.

22

The Great War

(1) CHAPTER OUTLINE

Edmund Arpin joins the army in 1917 less out of patriotism than out of a desire for excitement. In the Great War, he discovers that modern conflict is neither heroic nor noble. Nevertheless, his wartime adventures and the sense of common purpose he gains through his participation in the war effort make World War I a critical event in his life.

The Early War Years
   The Causes of War
   American Reactions
   The New Military Technology
   Difficulties of Neutrality
   World Trade and Neutrality Rights
   Intervening in Mexico and Central America

The United States Enters the War
   The Election of 1916
   Deciding for War
   A Patriotic Crusade
   Raising an Army

The Military Experience
   The American Doughboy
   The Black Soldier
   Over There

Domestic Impact of the War
   Financing the War
   Increasing Federal Power
   War Workers
   The Climax of Progressivism
   Suffrage for Women

Planning for Peace
   The Paris Peace Conference

Women for Peace
Wilson's Failed Dream

Conclusion: The Divided Legacy of the Great War

(2) SIGNIFICANT THEMES AND HIGHLIGHTS

1. As the anecdote about Edmund Arpin suggests, World War I affected the lives of Americans in many ways. Black and white soldiers helped make important contributions to victory. War brought new taxes and jobs, increased the power of the central government, and, as always, resulted in inflation.

2. The chapter explores American foreign policy before, during, and after the Great War. In these years, Wilson betrayed some of his democratic ideals and showed the basic continuity of American foreign policy by frequent interventions in Central America. When war broke out in Europe, Wilson's attempts to keep the country neutral were undermined by basic American sympathy for the Allies, economic ties with Great Britain and France, and U-boat incidents on the seas. Once at war, Wilson harbored dreams of a just peace. Although realizing some of his goals at the Versailles Peace Conference, Wilson was forced to make major concessions to the Allies, who did not share his idealistic vision of the world. He also lost the battle at home when the Senate refused to ratify the treaty.

3. The need for support in the election of 1916 prodded Wilson to promote various social reform measures advocated by progressives. Ironically, although reformers feared war, the war years represented the climax of the progressive movement. Once war was declared, the government carried on a gigantic propaganda campaign to persuade Americans of the war's noble purpose. These overzealous patriotic efforts led to violations of civil rights and antiforeign crusades at home.

(3) LEARNING GOALS

Familiarity with Basic Knowledge

After reading this chapter, you should be able to:

1. List four things that made American neutrality almost impossible.

2. Show how Wilson's policy toward Central America was an extension of both "big-stick" diplomacy and dollar diplomacy.

3. Explain why the Russian Revolution seemed to jeopardize Wilson's hopes for the postwar world.

4. Show the connections between the work of the Creel Committee and antiforeign and antiradical activities.

5. Compare the military experience of the United States with that of Great Britain and France.

Practice in Historical Thinking Skills

After reading this chapter, you should be able to:

1. Analyze how the war was, in an ironic sense, the climax of progressivism.

2. Assess Wilson's successes at the Versailles Peace Conference and his failures at home.

3. Analyze Wilson as a reluctant social reformer.

(4) IMPORTANT DATES AND NAMES TO KNOW

1914	Archduke Ferdinand assassinated
	World War I begins
	United States declares neutrality
	American troops invade Mexico and occupy Veracruz
1915	Germany announces submarine blockade of Great Britain
	Sinking of the *Lusitania*
	Arabic pledge
	Marines land in Haiti
1916	Army Reorganization Bill
	Expedition into Mexico
	Wilson reelected
	Workmen's Compensation Bill
	Keatings-Owen Child Labor Bill
	Federal Farm Loan Act
	National Women's party founded
1917	Germany resumes unrestricted submarine warfare
	United States breaks relations with Germany
	Zimmermann telegram
	Russian Revolution
	United States declares war on Germany
	War Revenue Act
	Espionage Act
	Committee on Public Information established
	Trading with the Enemy Act
	Selective Service Act

War Industries Board formed

1918	Sedition Act
	Flu epidemic sweeps nation
	Wilson's Fourteen Points
	American troops intervene in Russian Revolution

1918   Sedition Act
Flu epidemic sweeps nation
Wilson's Fourteen Points
American troops intervene in Russian Revolution

1919   Paris (Versailles) Peace Conference
Eighteenth Amendment prohibits alcoholic beverages
Senate rejects Treaty of Versailles

1920   Nineteenth Amendment grants women's suffrage

Other Names to Know

Victoriano Huerta
Louis Brandeis
Lenin (Vladimir Ilyich Ulyanov)
Carrie Chapman Catt
General John Pershing

Francisco "Pancho" Villa
George Creel
Bernard Baruch
Henry Cabot Lodge

(5) GLOSSARY OF IMPORTANT TERMS

Fourteen Points: Wilson's 1918 proposal for peace, which was an attempt to realize Western liberal and democratic principles in the postwar world; most dramatic was his call for a League of Nations

(6) ENRICHMENT IDEAS

1. There are many novels dealing with World War I that you may want to read. Some of the best known are Ernest Hemingway's *Farewell to Arms*, Erich Remarque's *All Quiet on the Western Front*, and John Dos Passos's *1919*.

2. You could investigate newspaper accounts of events like the sinking of the *Lusitania* to ascertain how "neutral" the American press was. Also check the editorial pages for articles and cartoons that suggest American sympathies. Magazines are also a good source for attitudes toward the war and may show the attempts to stir up patriotism.

(7) SAMPLE TEST AND EXAMINATION QUESTIONS

Multiple choice: Choose the best answer.

1. When war broke out in Europe in 1914,
   a. Jane Addams and others formed the Woman's Peace party
   b. hundreds joined ambulance units, the French Foreign Legion, and the Lafayette Espadrille
   c. many thought the Europeans had lost all reason
   d. all of the above

2. Full and complete American neutrality was difficult because of
   a. strong trade ties with the Central Powers
   b. the loyalties of central European immigrants to their native lands
   c. United States acceptance of British violations of international law
   d. Wilson's desire to give military support to the British

3. The U-boats created difficulties for international law because
   a. their goal was to sink American vessels
   b. international law demanded that ships be warned before attack, which defeated the purpose of submarine warfare
   c. of the *Sussex* pledge
   d. of none of the above

4. Wilson's vision of world order was based on his belief in
   a. free trade
   b. pluralism
   c. imperialism
   d. Marxism

5. Wilson refused to recognize the Huerta government because
   a. it took over American companies
   b. it favored rich landowners
   c. it was a dictatorship
   d. it attacked American troops in Veracruz

6. Wilson pushed for progressive reforms in 1916 primarily because
   a. he needed political support in an election year
   b. he believed that progressive goals were best for the country
   c. he thought reform would divert attention from the international crisis
   d. he needed to beat the Progressive party

7. The Russian Revolution threatened Wilson's hopes for world order because
   a. Kerensky refused to carry on the war against Germany
   b. Lenin rejected democracy and capitalism

c.   Lenin joined the Germans in fighting the Allies
d.   none of the above

8.   The Creel Committee
a.   organized American industry to fight the war
b.   created propaganda supporting the war effort
c.   brought Eugene Debs to trial for opposing the war
d.   set up training camps

9.   Most soldiers were
a.   high school graduates
b.   middle class
c.   illiterate
d.   from the lower classes

10. Black soldiers
a.   served in segregated units
b.   served mostly in combat units
c.   were immune from the draft
d.   refused to serve because of white racism

11. The war was financed in all of the following ways EXCEPT
a.   bonds
b.   taxes
c.   printing of paper money
d.   inflation

12. The women who worked during the war were characterized chiefly by being
a.   new to the work force
b.   married
c.   black
d.   unmarried

13. Women's suffrage was promoted during the war because
a.   Wilson was a longtime supporter
b.   both moderate and radical women's groups pressed their cause effectively
c.   working women threatened to strike unless they had the vote
d.   Elizabeth Cady Stanton persuaded Wilson of the political importance of women's votes

14. The Fourteen Points supported
a.   the Russian Revolution
b.   the United Nations
c.   freedom of the seas
d.   secret diplomacy

15. At Versailles, Wilson succeeded in
    a. gaining limited acceptance of the idea of self-determination
    b. blocking German reparations
    c. overturning the proposal for mandates
    d. persuading Henry Cabot Lodge to support the League of Nations

Essays

1. Senator George Norris said, "War brings no prosperity to the great mass of common patriotic citizens." To what extent is this an accurate assessment of the impact of World War I on American life?

2. Show how the war was, in an ironic sense, the climax of progressivism in its many forms.

3. World War I illustrated that the world's most powerful nations cannot easily remain either neutral or moral in a time of world conflict. Develop with evidence.

4. Wilson's failures in the postwar period were not as a diplomat but as a politician. Discuss, supporting your position with specific historical examples.

Identify and Interpret: Quotation
(that is, state who, what, where, when, and why significant)

The right of citizens of the United States to vote shall not be denied or abridged by the United States or by any State on account of sex.

WIRELESS COMMUNICATION

On the night of April 14, 1912, the *Titanic,* the largest ship ever built, hit an iceberg in the North Atlantic and sank in just over an hour. When the giant ship went down, it took more than 1,500 passengers to their deaths (651 were saved). While the stricken ship settled in the water, wireless operators on board sent out distress signals that were picked up by at least ten ships and a wireless station in Newfoundland. Only one of the ships was close enough to rescue passengers, but news of the disaster became headlines in the newspapers of Europe and America the next morning. Thanks to the wireless, millions of people received the news almost simultaneously, and they experienced a shared sense of loss.

Ships had been lost at sea almost from the beginning of history, but until the invention of the wireless, they usually just disappeared. A ship would be missing and then presumed lost, and no one would ever know the exact nature of the tragedy, since communication to other ships or shore was impossible. All types of messages traveled slowly. In the eighteenth century, it often took months for letters to cross the Atlantic, and distant events were reported in newspapers many weeks after they happened. The wireless helped to usher in an era of instant news, and it dramatically changed the way people perceived the world. The *New York Times* for April 21, 1912, commenting on the *Titanic* and the magic of the wireless, observed: "Night and day all the year round the millions upon the earth and the thousands upon the sea now reach out and grasp the thin air and use it as a thing more potent for human aid than any strand of wire or cable that was ever spun or woven."

Guglielmo Marconi invented the wireless in 1894, and less than a decade later, U.S. President Theodore Roosevelt and King Edward VII of Great Britain used it to exchange greetings across the Atlantic. By 1912, the wireless was a common, if not always predictable, form of international communication, linking ships to land in a system of instant communication. It joined the telegraph (1844) and the telephone (1876) in transforming communication and in making it possible to seem to be in two places at the same time. Marconi, who, like all great inventors, built on the work of others, succeeded in sending signals in Morse code over the invisible electromagnetic airwaves. Other experimenters soon successfully transmitted the human voice and music over the same waves. The wireless occupied a midpoint in the rising curve of technology that led to radio, television, the communications satellite, and computers.

The wireless and the radio made ocean travel much safer and war more efficient by improving communications between ships at sea and among army units on the ground. Within a decade after the *Titanic* disaster, technology also transformed American lives in direct and subtle ways. Weather forecasting became more accurate and timely, providing ample warning to farmers and ordinary citizens about approaching storms. News of battles, elections, sporting events, and disasters both domestic and foreign traveled over the airwaves. This instant news could have very practical ramifications, influencing decisions in everything from business matters to whether or not to wear a coat to work. But in a broader sense, it made all Americans citizens of the world. The news of the end of World War I in 1918, the attack on Pearl Harbor in 1941, and the walk on the moon in 1969 united millions of people worldwide and made them participants in the events. The new communications technology and instant news, symbolized by the wireless and its role in spreading the word about the sinking of the *Titanic,* made twentieth-century Americans very different from those who lived before them.

23

Affluence and Anxiety

(1) CHAPTER OUTLINE

Two black Alabama sharecroppers, John and Lizzie Parker, move north during World War I in search of jobs, opportunity, a home of their own, and education for their children. Eventually they reach Detroit, with its promise of wartime jobs in the automotive industry. As the decade of the 1920s develops, the Parkers experience racial hatred; uncertain, part-time work; a half-finished house on an unpaved ghetto street; and a completed high school degree for their daughter Sally.

Postwar Problems
Red Scare
Working-Class Protest
Ku Klux Klan
The Sacco-Vanzetti Case
Religious Intolerance

A Prospering Economy
The Rising Standard of Living
The Rise of the Modern Corporation
Electrification
Automobile Culture
The Exploding Metropolis
A Communications Revolution

Hopes Raised, Promises Deferred
Clash of Values
Religious Fundamentalism
Immigration and Migration
Marcus Garvey: Black Messiah
The Harlem Renaissance and the Lost Generation
Women Struggle for Equality
Rural America in the 1920s
The Workers' Share of Prosperity

The Business of Politics
> Harding and Coolidge
> Herbert Hoover
> Foreign Policy in the 1920s
> The Survival of Progressivism
> Temperance Triumphant
> The Election of 1928
> Stock Market Crash

Conclusion: A New Era of Prosperity and Problems

(2) SIGNIFICANT THEMES AND HIGHLIGHTS

1. The dominant theme of the decade of the 1920s, as the Parkers' story suggests, was the mixed fulfillment of various dreams of suburban comfort and success. In a decade in which general prosperity, quick riches in the stock market, and new technologies held out the promise of success to all, many, like John and Lizzie Parker, found their dreams always just out of reach.

2. The 1920s, neatly packed between the end of World War I and the stock market crash in 1929, was a decade of paradox and contradiction. Conflicting trends persisted throughout the decade: prosperity and poverty, optimism and disillusionment, inventiveness and intolerance, flamboyant heroism and fallen idols, anxiety and affluence. Many Americans, like the Parkers and the New Era decade itself, saw their hopes raised and then deferred or dashed.

3. This chapter illustrates the profound effects that technological developments (the automobile, radio, the bathroom, for example) have on diverse aspects of people's lives.

4. Interwoven throughout the chapter are the hopes and fears of many different groups--blacks in northern cities, migrant Mexicans and other immigrants, nativist Americans in the Ku Klux Klan and other patriotic organizations, women, white suburbanites, factory workers, sports and media heroes, disillusioned writers, temperance crusaders, optimistic investors and advertisers, and many others.

(3) LEARNING GOALS

Familiarity with Basic Knowledge

After reading this chapter, you should be able to:

1. Describe the postwar mood in America and the strikes, race riots, and Palmer raids of 1919 and 1920.

2. Name several technological inventions and influential ideas of the New Era and their impact on social and economic life.

3. Outline the development, distribution, and discrepancies of prosperity in the 1920s.

4. Describe the presidential styles and administrations of Harding and Coolidge.

5. Outline the foreign policy currents of the United States during the 1920s.

6. Describe the election of 1928 and the stock market crash.

Practice in Historical Thinking Skills

After reading this chapter, you should be able to:

1. Analyze and evaluate the distribution of the benefits of prosperity during the New Era.

2. Analyze the impact of the automobile and other technological developments on American social and economic life in the 1920s.

3. Explain the major paradoxes and contradictions of the 1920s.

(4) IMPORTANT DATES AND NAMES TO KNOW

1900 - 1930	Electricity powers the "second industrial revolution"
1917	Race riot in East St. Louis, Illinois
1918	World War I ends
1919	Treaty of Versailles Strikes in Seattle, Boston, and elsewhere Red Scare and Palmer raids Race riots in Chicago and other cities Marcus Garvey's United Negro Improvement Association spreads
1920	Warren G. Harding elected president Women vote in national elections First commercial radio broadcast Sacco and Vanzetti arrested Sinclair Lewis, *Main Street*

1921	Immigration Quota Law
	Disarmament Conference
	First birth control conference
	Sheppard-Towner Maternity Act

1921 - 1922   Postwar depression

1922   Fordney-McCumber Tariff
Sinclair Lewis, *Babbitt*

1923   Harding dies; Calvin Coolidge becomes president
Teapot Dome scandal

1924   Coolidge reelected president
Peak of Ku Klux Klan activity
Immigration Quota Law

1925   Scopes trial in Dayton, Tennessee
F. Scott Fitzgerald, *The Great Gatsby*
Bruce Barton, *The Man Nobody Knows*
Alain Locke, *The New Negro*
Claude McKay, *Home to Harlem*
5 million enameled bathroom fixtures produced

1926   Ernest Hemingway, *The Sun Also Rises*

1927   National Origins Act
McNary-Haugen Farm Relief Bill
Sacco and Vanzetti executed
Lindbergh flies solo, New York to Paris
First talking movie, *The Jazz Singer*
Henry Ford produces his 15 millionth car

1928   Herbert Hoover elected president
Kellogg-Briand Treaty
Stock market soars

1929   27 million registered cars in United States
10 million households own radios
100 million people attend movies
Stock market crash

Other Names to Know

John Reed
William J. Simmons
Margaret Sanger
John L. Lewis
Babe Ruth
John Scopes
Langston Hughes
Charles Evans Hughes
Al Smith

A. Mitchell Palmer
H. L. Mencken
Marcus Garvey
Al Capone
Aimee Semple McPherson
Clarence Darrow
Andrew Mellon
Charles Dawes
Billy Sunday

(5) GLOSSARY OF IMPORTANT TERMS

"second industrial revolution": the shift in American industry from the production of manufactured goods for other producers (such as coal and steel) to those for consumers (such as synthetic fabrics, chemicals, and petroleum)

(6) ENRICHMENT IDEAS

1. Examine the advertisements in some magazines of the 1920s to see how they reflect the currents of American culture. What do they suggest about attitudes toward blacks, women, and other groups? What do they reveal about American values and priorities? Now look at any contemporary magazine, watch television, and observe current advertisements. What do you learn about today's attitudes, values, and priorities? What has changed? What has not?

2. It would be quite easy to read some newspapers from the 1920s, either the *New York Times* or a local newspaper (both of which your library probably has on microfilm). You might focus on the coverage of the Teapot Dome scandal, the Scopes trial, Lindbergh's flight, or the election of 1928. Or you might look at advertising, editorials, and various feature articles to capture the mood of the 1920s.

3. One way to experience the currents of social life during the 1920s is through reading the literature of the time. Such novels as F. Scott Fitzgerald's *The Great Gatsby* and *Tender Is the Night;* Ernest Hemingway's *The Sun Also Rises;* Sherwood Anderson's *Winesburg, Ohio;* Sinclair Lewis's *Main Street, Babbitt,* and *Elmer Gantry*; Claude McKay's *Home to Harlem;* Jean Toomer's *Cane;* John Dos Passos's *1919* and *The Big Money;* William Faulkner's *The Sound and the Fury;* Theodore Dreiser's *An American Tragedy;* and many others provide wonderful insights into manners and morals. Select one of these, or another novel written in and about the 1920s, read it, and write an essay about how well it reflects the times.

(7) SAMPLE TEST AND EXAMINATION QUESTIONS

Multiple choice: Choose the best answer.

1. The postwar mood in America was characterized by all of the following EXCEPT
   a. race riots and strikes
   b. an end to wartime enthusiasm
   c. an increase in immigrants from Russia
   d. the rise of the Ku Klux Klan

2. The steel workers' strike in 1919 was caused primarily by
   a. poor wages and long hours of work
   b. workers' pressures for a cost-of-living clause in their contracts
   c. resentment over hiring black workers
   d. Bolshevik influence in steel unions

3. The Red Scare and Palmer raids
   a. removed a serious Communist threat from the United States
   b. inspired a general strike in Seattle
   c. led to Palmer's death when his house was bombed
   d. represented one of the biggest violations of civil liberties in American history

4. Most members of the Ku Klux Klan opposed all of the following EXCEPT
   a. Catholics
   b. the League of Nations
   c. prohibition
   d. unrestricted immigration

5. The "second industrial revolution" produced goods primarily for
   a. the steel and coal industries
   b. other producers
   c. consumers
   d. war-torn Europeans

6. The automobile led to all of the following EXCEPT
   a. the growth of suburbs
   b. the rise of installment credit plans
   c. an increase in prostitution
   d. the growth of the petroleum industry

7. Henry Ford was
   a. a champion of the unionization of auto workers
   b. the inventor of the assembly line
   c. a ruthless industrialist in pressuring others to abide by his will
   d. a progressive industrialist who introduced labor reforms into his company

69

8. The immigration quota laws of 1921 and 1924 did all of the following EXCEPT
   a. limit the number of immigrants from southern and eastern Europe
   b. put a lower quota on immigrants from Germany and Great Britain
   c. open the country to Puerto Rican and Mexican laborers
   d. virtually ban Asian immigrants

9. Religious fundamentalists of the 1920s
   a. were Baptists
   b. did not participate in advances in technology to spread their word
   c. only believed certain parts of the Bible were true
   d. rejected modernism, pluralism, and the social gospel

10. Marcus Garvey was an admirer of
    a. Booker T. Washington
    b. W. E. B. Du Bois
    c. Malcolm X
    d. all of the above

11. Writers of the Harlem Renaissance and the Lost Generation were disillusioned with all of the following EXCEPT
    a. the loss of idealism from World War I
    b. materialistic, business-dominated American society
    c. the conformity and prejudice of American life
    d. new social and lifestyle freedoms

12. Women's lives in the 1920s changed because of
    a. labor-saving devices which reduced the time spent on housework
    b. vast new workplace opportunities
    c. an end to the sexual double standard
    d. some increased sexual freedom

13. Under Secretary of the Treasury Andrew Mellon, individual and corporate taxes during the 1920s
    a. were substantially reduced
    b. were increased slightly
    c. remained at wartime levels
    d. none of the above

14. The Washington Conference
    a. lowered tariffs

b. dealt with the tangle of war debts
c. achieved a measure of disarmament
d. did all of the above

15. The Sheppard-Towner Maternity Act was promoted and supported by
    a. the American Medical Association
    b. the Children's Bureau
    c. the feminist caucus in Congress
    d. the Right to Life movement

Essays

1. The 1920s was a decade of contradiction and paradox. Discuss.

2. Do you think the decade of the 1920s was one in which the American people looked more to the past or to the future? Or did they look in both directions at once? Explain.

3. Analyze the impact of the automobile and other technological developments on American social and economic life in the 1920s.

4. Analyze and evaluate who benefited from the prosperity of the 1920s and who did not.

5. Which of the following persons best typifies the American character in the 1920s: Henry Ford, Charles Lindbergh, Herbert Hoover, John Parker, or F. Scott Fitzgerald? Or would you pick someone else? Give reasons for your choice.

24

The Great Depression and the New Deal

(1) CHAPTER OUTLINE

The Depression changed Diana Morgan's life, as it did the lives of countless other Americans. It disrupted her comfortable existence and forced her to search for work in order to help her family. Diana's job in a New Deal agency introduced her to the far more serious problems of other Americans and persuaded her of the importance of New Deal efforts in alleviating misery and want.

The Great Depression
   The Depression Begins
   Hoover and the Great Depression
   The Collapsing Economy
   The Bonus Army

Roosevelt and the First New Deal
   The Election of 1932
   The Cabinet and the "Brain Trust"

One Hundred Days
   The Banking Crisis
   Relief Measures
   Agricultural Adjustment Act
   Industrial Recovery
   Civilian Conservation Corps
   Tennessee Valley Authority
   Critics of the New Deal

The Second New Deal
   Work Relief and Social Security
   Aiding the Farmers
   The Dust Bowl: An Ecological Disaster
   The New Deal and the West
   Controlling Corporate Power and Taxing the Wealthy
   The New Deal for Labor
   America's Minorities in the 1930s
   Women and the New Deal

The Last Years of the New Deal
 The Election of 1936
 The Battle of the Supreme Court
 The Third New Deal

The Other Side of the 1930s
 Taking to the Road
 The Electric Home
 The Age of Leisure
 Literary Reflections of the 1930s
 Radio's Finest Hour
 The Silver Screen

Conclusion: The Ambivalence of the Great Depression

(2) SIGNIFICANT THEMES AND HIGHLIGHTS

1. As the anecdote about Diana Morgan suggests, the Depression decade was a harsh one for many Americans. Although Hoover moved forcefully to meet the crisis, he failed to stop the economic decline or to gain the confidence of the American people.

2. Although Franklin Roosevelt built on Hoover's beginning, unlike Hoover, he was able to persuade Americans that his programs could solve the country's economic woes. Some characterized his programs as radical, but Roosevelt steered a moderate course with both his recovery measures and his efforts at social justice and reform. He never succeeded, however, in bringing the country out of the Depression.

3. The chapter shows the more positive side of the Depression era. Middle-class Americans were caught up in a communications revolution, enjoyed spectator sports, were fascinated by gadgets, and were interested in travel. The 1930s was a decade defined by the modern kitchen and Walt Disney just as much as by bread lines and alphabet-soup agencies. This bright side of the 1930s suggests how hard it is to generalize about a complex period like the Depression.

(3) LEARNING GOALS

Familiarity with Basic Knowledge

After reading this chapter, you should be able to:

1. Give three reasons for the deepening economic depression and three measures Hoover took to stem the Depression.

2. Characterize the first New Deal from 1933 to 1935 and name several measures of relief, recovery, and reform passed in the first hundred days.

3. Show how the Social Security Act and the Works Progress Administration exemplified the move of the second New Deal toward goals of social reform and social justice.

4. Explain the significance of the Wagner Act (National Labor Relations Act) and its impact on organized labor.

5. Characterize the New Deal's programs for minority groups.

6. Give three or four examples of the "other side" of the 1930s.

Practice in Historical Thinking Skills

After reading this chapter, you should be able to:

1. Compare and contrast Hoover's and Roosevelt's approaches to the Depression.

2. Evaluate the New Deal as the realization of progressive dreams.

3. Develop an argument supporting or rejecting the chapter author's assessment of the New Deal: "It promoted social justice and social reform, but it provided very little for those at the bottom of American society."

(4) IMPORTANT DATES AND NAMES TO KNOW

1929	Stock market crashes Agricultural Marketing Act
1930	Depression worsens Hawley-Smoot Tariff
1932	Reconstruction Finance Corporation established Federal Home Loan Banking Act Glass-Steagall Banking Act Federal Emergency Relief Act Bonus march on Washington Franklin D. Roosevelt elected president
1933	Emergency Banking Relief Act Home Owners Loan Corporation Twenty-first Amendment repeals Eighteenth Amendment (prohibition) Agricultural Adjustment Act

National Industrial Recovery Act (NIRA)
Civilian Conservation Corps (CCC) established
Tennessee Valley Authority (TVA) established
Public Works Administration established

1934 Unemployment peaks
Federal Housing Administration (FHA) established
Indian Reorganization Act

1935 Second New Deal begins
Works Progress Administration (WPA) established
Social Security Act
Rural Electrification Act
National Labor Relations (Wagner-Connery) Act
Public Utility Holding Company Act
Committee for Industrial Organization (CIO) formed

1936 United Auto Workers sit-down strikes against General Motors
Roosevelt reelected president
Economy begins to rebound

1937 Attempt to expand the Supreme Court
Economic collapse
Farm Security Administration established
National Housing Act

1938 Fair Labor Standards Act
Agricultural Adjustment Act

1939 John Steinbeck, *The Grapes of Wrath*
Margaret Mitchell, *Gone With the Wind*

Other Names to Know

Francis E. Townshend	Father Charles E. Coughlin
Huey Long	John L. Lewis
Mary McLeod Bethune	John Maynard Keynes
Frances Perkins	Dorothea Lange

(5) GLOSSARY OF IMPORTANT TERMS

deficit spending: the practice of having the government spend more dollars on goods and services than it receives from taxes and other revenues in order to stimulate the economy

Brain Trust: FDR's informal group of advisers

(6) ENRICHMENT IDEAS

1. Enjoy some 1930s movies as historical documents. What do they tell you about the myths, values, and spirit of that decade?

2. Your community may well have a mural painted by the WPA or a park constructed by the CCC. Locate and visit the site to see the kinds of work the government subsidized. What contributions to your community were made by these programs? Similarly, your library probably has a state guide written by WPA teams. Find it and see what kinds of historical and cultural sites were described.

3. In addition to Studs Terkel's *Hard Times,* a superb oral history of the 1930s, your library may have interesting local collections of primary documents that capture personal responses to the Depression years. You can use them in the same way as you might use the material collected from interviewing family and friends.

4. For a picture of the life of migrant workers in the 1930s, you could read the novel mentioned in the text, John Steinbeck's *The Grapes of Wrath.* For the Depression experience of blacks in the South, see Zora Neale Hurston's *Their Eyes Are Watching God,* and for black migrants in northern cities, read Richard Wright's *Native Son.*

(7) SAMPLE TEST AND EXAMINATION QUESTIONS

Multiple choice: Choose the best answer.

1. In 1929, Hoover did all of the following EXCEPT
    a. tell the American people to be optimistic
    b. declare a bank holiday
    c. support a tax cut
    d. urge businessmen to keep employment and wages up

2. During the 1930s,
    a. American family size remained stable
    b. the number of divorces rose
    c. the marriage rate dropped
    d. family size increased slightly

3. Hoover believed that the federal government must combat the economic collapse through
    a. direct subsidies
    b. relief to the unemployed

    c. loans to business and individuals
    d. the curtailment of agricultural production

4. Early New Deal measures included all of the following EXCEPT
    a. banking legislation
    b. attempts to reduce government spending
    c. relief measures
    d. Social Security

5. The Agricultural Adjustment Act
    a. paid farmers to reduce acreage
    b. helped small farmers more than large farmers
    c. was welcomed by farmer leaders and economists
    d. resulted in more food for those on relief

6. Social Security
    a. covered most workers
    b. was financed entirely through taxes on businesses
    c. included all married women workers
    d. levied a regressive tax on workers' wages

7. The Wagner Act did all of the following EXCEPT
    a. support labor's right to organize
    b. support the right to bargain collectively
    c. require workers to join unions
    d. establish a labor relations board

8. The sit-down strike was
    a. a tactic that involved occupying factory buildings
    b. picketing inside factory gates rather than outside
    c. a way of provoking violent confrontations with management
    d. a tactic ordered by union Communist leaders

9. During the New Deal, Roosevelt
    a. made sure blacks received benefits equal to those of whites
    b. relied on the "black cabinet" for advice on racial matters
    c. supported an antilynching bill
    d. pushed for a constitutional amendment to abolish the poll tax

10. The Indian Reorganization Act
    a. granted citizenship to all Indians born in U.S.
    b. tried to restore the political independence of tribes
    c. allowed gambling on Indian reservations
    d. encouraged Indians to assimilate

11. In the 1930s,
    a. fewer women were appointed to high government positions than under Hoover
    b. feminism declined
    c. women were more affected by economic collapse than men
    d. more women lost their jobs than did men

12. The CIO
    a. separated workers by skill and craft
    b. excluded women
    c. excluded blacks
    d. organized workers on an industrywide basis

13. During the 1930s, blacks
    a. stayed mainly in the South
    b. continued to migrate to the North
    c. found new jobs and security through government programs
    d. stayed loyal to the party of Lincoln

14. New Deal housing legislation
    a. dramatically improved the housing of the poor
    b. helped the middle class by ensuring long-term mortgages
    c. helped the middle class fix up their urban houses
    d. gave subsidies to homebuilders

15. The New Deal
    a. led to a significant redistribution of wealth
    b. redistributed power slightly through the Wagner Act
    c. undercut the power of business significantly
    d. none of the above

Essays

1. Items 1-3 in the "Learning Goals" section "Practice in Historical Thinking Skills" lend themselves to topics for practicing writing essays.

2. "Although the Depression shook faith in the American dream, the New Deal was based on a reaffirmation of that dream." Discuss.

3. "Cries that the New Deal was too radical were off target. The New Deal shored up and rationalized the capitalist system." Discuss the extent to which you agree with this assessment.

4. "The New Deal was little more than warmed-up progressivism." Do you agree? Why or why not?

Alphabet Soup: The New Deal passed so much legislation and introduced so many new government agencies that we have learned to identify many American agencies and organizations by their acronyms. How many of the following can you identify?

1.ICC_____

2.AAA_____

3.CIO_____

4.NIRA_____

5.NAACP _____

6.CCC_____

7.FERA_____

8.TVA_____

9.NLRB_____

10.FDIC_____

Identify and Interpret: Quotation
(that is, state who, what, where, when, and why significant)

I am prepared under my constitutional duty to recommend the measures that a stricken nation in the midst of a stricken world may require. These measures, or such other measures as the Congress may build out of its experience and wisdom, I shall seek, within my constitutional authority, to bring to speedy adoption.

But in the event that the Congress shall fail to take one of these two courses, and in the event that the national emergency is still critical, I shall not evade the clear course of duty that will then confront me. I shall ask the Congress for the one remaining instrument to meet the crisis--broad executive power to wage a war against the emergency as great as the power that would be given me if we were in fact invaded by a foreign foe.

25

World War II

(1) CHAPTER OUTLINE

N. Scott Momaday, a Kiowa Indian, grows up during World War II playing games, listening to the radio, and going to movies and football games. The presence of war colors his childhood, however. The games he and his friends play are war games, his parents are both employed because of the war, and he is dismayed when others often mistake him for the Japanese enemy.

The Twisting Road to War
> Foreign Policy in the 1930s
> Neutrality in Europe
> Ethiopia and Spain
> War in Europe
> The Election of 1940
> Lend-Lease
> The Path to Pearl Harbor

The Home Front
> Mobilizing for War
> Patriotic Fervor
> Internment of Japanese-Americans
> African and Hispanic Americans at War

Social Impact of the War
> Wartime Opportunities
> Women Workers for Victory
> Entertaining the People
> The GIs' War
> Women in Uniform

A War of Diplomats and Generals
> War Aims
> 1942: Year of Disaster
> A Strategy for Ending the War
> The Invasion of Europe
> The Politics of Victory
> The Big Three at Yalta
> The Atomic Age Begins

Conclusion: Peace, Prosperity, and International Responsibilities

(2) SIGNIFICANT THEMES AND HIGHLIGHTS

1. Although the United States tried to stand apart from the international crises of the 1930s, some of its policies actually assisted Franco and Mussolini. As war broke out in Europe, the United States hesitantly, but predictably, began to assist Great Britain. It was the Japanese attack at Pearl Harbor, however, that made the American involvement in the war official.

2. The American economy finally emerged from its years of depression to produce the equipment and supplies that won the war. The war touched people's lives by uprooting them from their homes, by providing them with jobs, by heightening their sense of patriotism, by both attacking and adding to racial discrimination, and by affecting family patterns. Even the ways in which Americans spent their leisure time bore the imprint of war, as Scott Momaday's childhood games suggest.

3. The United States never formulated specific war goals beyond the obvious one of defeating the enemy as rapidly as possible. The alliance that was necessary for victory was quickly strained by the delay in opening a second front in Europe. In 1945, with victory within reach, serious disagreements about the future of the world began to surface. The explosion of the world's first atomic bomb added a new and frightening element to world diplomacy.

(3) LEARNING GOALS

Familiarity with Basic Knowledge

After reading this chapter, you should be able to:

1. Describe the response of the United States to the Ethiopian crisis, the Spanish civil war, and Japanese aggression in China.

2. Show how wartime government agencies and boards helped to turn America's economy to wartime goals.

3. Explain the reasons for the internment of Japanese-Americans and contrast that policy with that toward Italian-Americans and German-Americans.

4. Assess the economic impact of the war on black and Hispanic-Americans and women.

5. Describe the political and diplomatic concerns that became important at the war's end, especially the controversy over opening a second front, and explain the agreements the United States and the Soviet Union reached at Yalta.

Practice in Historical Thinking Skills

After reading this chapter, you should be able to:

1. Explain why the United States used the atomic bomb and evaluate the decision militarily, diplomatically, and morally.

2. Compare the efforts to whip up patriotic feeling in World War II with similar efforts in World War I and assess the effectiveness and consequences in each case.

3. Discuss racism and attitudes toward women as a part of the American wartime experience.

(4) IMPORTANT DATES AND NAMES TO KNOW

1931 - 1932	Japan seizes Manchuria
1933	Adolph Hitler becomes chancellor of Germany United States recognizes the Soviet Union Roosevelt extends Good Neighbor policy
1934	Germany begins rearmament
1935	Italy invades Ethiopia First Neutrality Act
1936	Spanish civil war begins Second Neutrality Act Roosevelt reelected
1937	Third Neutrality Act
1938	Hitler annexes Austria, occupies Sudetenland German persecution of Jews intensifies
1939	Nazi-Soviet Pact German invasion of Poland; World War II begins
1940	Roosevelt elected for a third term Selective Service Act
1941	FDR's "Four Freedoms" speech Proposed black march on Washington Executive order outlaws discrimination in defense industries

Lend-Lease Act
Germany attacks Russia
Japanese assets in United States frozen
Japanese attack Pearl Harbor; United States declares war on Japan
Germany declares war on the United States

1942   Internment of Japanese-Americans
Second Allied front in Africa launched

1943   Invasion of Sicily
Italian campaign; Italy surrenders
United Mine Workers strike
Race riots in Detroit and other cities

1944   Normandy Invasion (Operation Overlord)
Congress passes GI Bill
Roosevelt elected for a fourth term

1945   Yalta conference
Roosevelt dies; Harry S Truman becomes president
Germany surrenders
Successful test of atomic bomb
Hiroshima and Nagasaki bombed; Japan surrenders

Other Names to Know

Senator Gerald Nye	Benito Mussolini
Joseph Stalin	Winston Churchill
J. Robert Oppenheimer	Dwight Eisenhower

(5) GLOSSARY OF IMPORTANT TERMS

blitzkrieg: sudden and extensive German military assault and invasion accompanied by massive air strikes

nisei: Japanese born in the United States

issei: Japanese born in Japan and ineligible for citizenship

Operation Overlord: code name for the amphibious invasion of France

(6) ENRICHMENT IDEAS

1. As *Recovering The Past* for this chapter shows, World War II offers you the chance to interview family and friends about their wartime experiences. Remember to ask about the home front as well as the experiences of those who went overseas and were engaged in battles. You might try to the following basic questions: How were you affected by the war? What is your most vivid memory? In what ways did the war affect your generation? How do you think your generation differs from the present one?

2. Family photograph albums are also sources of information about your family's past during the war. Find some photographs to show how people lived during wartime and how the war affected family relationships.

3. Popular music and magazines like *Life* and *Time* can also provide clues to the mood of the 1940s. How did the war affect song lyrics and the news magazines? What appeals were made to women listeners and readers? to children? to the old? What about people of color?

(7) SAMPLE TEST AND EXAMINATION QUESTIONS

Multiple choice: Choose the best answer.

1. By recognizing Russia, the United States wanted
    a. to recognize the validity of communism
    b. to find an ally against the growing might of Germany
    c. to gain a market for surplus American grain
    d. to facilitate the flight of Jews from the Soviet Union

2. Senator Gerald Nye's committee investigation sought to prove that
    a. World War I had resulted from economic ties with the Allies
    b. pacifism was dangerous for the United States
    c. tariffs should be raised
    d. the United States should reverse its policy toward Latin America

3. During the Ethiopian crisis and the Spanish civil war, the United States
    a. tried to help the League of Nations stop hostilities
    b. thought that the League was inflating what were only minor incidents
    c. actually assisted Mussolini and Franco in achieving their goals
    d. stood aside and did nothing

4. During the 1930s, Japan
   a. invaded Manchuria
   b. invaded China
   c. hoped to replace white imperial regimes in the Far East
   d. all of the above

5. The Americans were surprised by the attack on Pearl Harbor because
   a. they thought economic sanctions would prevent war
   b. they were tricked by misleading messages in Japanese code
   c. they thought the Japanese were too busy fighting in China to launch an attack in the Pacific
   d. they expected an attack elsewhere

6. Taxation paid for what percentage of the war's cost?
   a. 10 percent
   b. 23 percent
   c. 40 percent
   d. 70 percent

7. American policy toward Japanese-Americans was
   a. one of watchful waiting
   b. one of internment
   c. similar to the policy toward other groups
   d. nonexistent because Americans were not worried about such a small number of people

8. During the war, blacks
   a. succeeded in pressuring the government to support nondiscriminatory hiring in defense and government jobs
   b. remained largely in the South, moving into southern cities
   c. experienced decreasing discrimination
   d. all of the above

9. During the war, women
   a. took jobs in heavy industry
   b. earned wages similar to men's
   c. managed to break the notion that a woman's place was in the home
   d. entered the professions in great numbers

10. After the war, women workers
    a. were encouraged to stay on the job until the economy recovered
    b. joined unions and fought to stay at work
    c. were dismissed twice as often as were men
    d. none of the above

11. Roosevelt's war aims were
    a. clearly defined
    b. never explained
    c. concealed
    d. imprecise

12. In 1942,
    a. Churchill was in favor of relying on bombing raids to subdue Germany
    b. Stalin pressed for a second front in Europe
    c. Roosevelt agreed to an Allied offensive
    d. all of the above

13. At Yalta, FDR
    a. agreed that the Russians should liberate Berlin
    b. won the Soviets' promise to help win the Pacific war
    c. revealed to the Soviets that the Americans were working on an atomic bomb
    d. promised to open a second front

14. Truman and others decided to use the atomic bomb against Japan because
    a. they believed that the Japanese would collapse because of such a show of power
    b. they wanted to knock Japan out of the war so that they could finish off Germany
    c. they wanted to impress the Soviet Union with American power
    d. they thought that only by dropping the bomb could they force the Japanese to give up their emperor

15. The atomic bomb was dropped on
    a. a military site
    b. a site where few Japanese lived
    c. one city and one military site
    d. two cities without military significance

Identify and show a relationship between each of the following pairs.

Nye Committee	*and*	Neutrality Acts
Ethiopia	*and*	Spain
Atlantic Charter	*and*	Yalta
March on Washington	*and*	Rosie the Riveter
Pearl Harbor	*and*	Hiroshima

Essays

1. World War II has been called the "last good war." Write an essay indicating what you think that statement means and the extent to which you agree with it.

2. During the 1930s, the foreign policy of the United States was aimed at preventing American involvement in World War II. Discuss.

3. Although the Cold War is often thought to have begun after World War II, one can see it emerging during the war. To what extent do you agree or disagree with this statement?

4. Wars often instigate more important social changes than social reform movements. Does this statement characterize the war experience in the United States?

5. Should the United States have used the atomic bomb in August 1945? Why or why not?

Identify and Interpret: Cartoon
(that is, state who, what, where, when, and why significant)

LETTING THE GENIE OUT OF THE BOTTLE

A RESILIENT PEOPLE
1945 - 1997

The final section of *The American People* traces the recent history of the United States and highlights themes developed earlier in the text. We will explore the sense of mission the Cold War inspired with the former Soviet Union and the tensions between the United States's efforts to support and spread democratic institutions and its pursuit of economic gain. We will trace the resilience of the federal government as it accepted more responsibility for promoting the well-being of its citizens by extending the boundaries of the welfare state in the years after World War II. As American life became increasingly bureaucratized and regulated, a reaction against the role of government set in, building all the way through the Bush administration. Finally, we will examine the continuing struggle to realize national ideals of liberty and equality in racial, gender, and social relations as new waves of immigration from Latin America and Asia increased the diversity of the American people.

Chapters 26 and 27 are paired. Chapter 26, "Postwar Growth and Social Change," describes the expansion of self-interest in an age of extensive material growth but also shows how economic development promoted new patterns of regulation that transformed American life. Chapter 27, "Chills and Fever During the Cold War," shows how the United States moved from an uneasy friendship with the Soviet Union to disillusionment and hostility. The Cold War shaped American policy around the world and also had a pronounced domestic impact as the nation faced a second Red Scare in the late 1940s and early 1950s. Cold War assumptions led directly to Vietnam.

Chapter 28, "High Water and Ebb Tide of Liberalism," traces the development of the welfare state in the 1940s and 1950s then describes the debate in the 1960s and 1970s over the appropriate role of government. It reveals how both political parties accepted the need for greater federal activity in order to ensure the liberty and welfare of all citizens. The Kennedy-Johnson years in the 1960s marked a highwater era of liberalism that was soon lost in the emerging Republican majority and in the turn away from liberalism under Nixon and Ford.

Chapter 29, "The Struggle for Social Reform," examines the reform impulse of the 1960s and 1970s. With roots in the earliest days of American society, this effort required struggle on the part of blacks, women, Latinos, Native Americans, and others who sought to achieve the long-deferred American dream.

In Chapter 30, "The Revival of Conservatism," we explore the severe economic crises and demographic transformations in the 1980s and '90s, years marked by the conservative Reagan Revolution, continued under Bush until the election of William Jefferson Clinton in 1992. The chapter—and text—concludes with a look at America's place in a world of collapsed communism and growing ethnic, national, and multicultural rivalries.

26

Postwar Growth and Social Change

(1) CHAPTER OUTLINE

Ray Kroc starts the McDonald's drive-in hamburger chain in 1954 and makes a fortune, capitalizing on the conformist suburban American desire for the security and standardization represented by the bland fast-food hamburger. His success symbolizes the fulfillment of one version of the American dream.

Economic Boom
> The Thriving Peacetime Economy
> The Corporate Impact on American Life
> Changing Work Patterns
> The Union Movement at High Tide
> Agricultural Workers in Trouble

Demographic and Technological Trends
> Population Shifts
> The New Suburbs
> The Environmental Impact
> Technology Supreme
> The Consumer Culture

Consensus and Conformity
> Conformity in School and Religious Life
> Back to the Kitchen
> Cultural Rebels

The Other America
> Poverty amid Affluence
> Hard Times for African-Americans
> Minorities on the Fringe

Conclusion: Qualms amid Affluence

(2) SIGNIFICANT THEMES AND HIGHLIGHTS

1. Ray Kroc's success with McDonald's almost perfectly suggests the domestic themes and social emphases of American life in the 1950s—the importance of the automobile, bland fast-food meals, and profitable franchises to standardize life. As symbolized by McDonald's, uniformity, conformity, materialism, and suburban security were the hallmarks of America in the 1950s.

2. This triumph of material self-interest was a white middle-class phenomenon. The experience of blacks, Native Americans, and Hispanics showed the limits of economic growth and of social policy in a conservative age.

3. An economic boom in a more highly structured era of social and technological change dominated the tone of the age. This chapter shows how such social phenomena as television, advertising, the birthrate, studies of sexual behavior, and clothing, as well as fast-food chains, can be used to understand the character of an age.

(3) LEARNING GOALS

Familiarity with Basic Knowledge

After reading this chapter, you should be able to:

1. Describe the postwar economic boom and its effects in the corporate world, workers' world, and agricultural world, as well as on the environment.

2. Describe the demographic growth patterns of the United States in the postwar years and state the appeal of suburban living and the automobile for the American people.

3. Give some examples of cultural conformity in the 1950s, particularly in women's lives, and describe the values espoused by cultural rebels.

4. Give some examples of challenges to that culture of conformity.

5. Describe five economic developments of the 1950s and explain both the importance of the auto industry and the pattern of business concentration.

6. Describe the lives of those who did not benefit from this period of affluence.

7. Characterize the religious life of America in the 1950s.

8. Describe the consumer culture of the 1950s, the ways the media promoted it, and some of the results.

Practice in Historical Thinking Skills

After reading this chapter, you should be able to:

1. Analyze the social implications of the economic boom and population shifts in postwar American society.

2. Identify the roots of some enduring trends of contemporary American society.

3. Assess the gains and losses of groups in "the other America" in the postwar years.

(4) IMPORTANT DATES AND NAMES TO KNOW

1944	GI Bill passed
1945	World War II ends Wave of strikes in heavy industries
1946	Truman vetoes bill extending Office of Price Administration Prices rise by 25 percent in 18 months Union strikes in the auto, coal, steel, and electrical industries Employment Act Benjamin Spock's *Baby and Child Care*
1947	Taft-Hartley Act Jackie Robinson breaks the color line in major-league baseball
1948	Executive order bars racial discrimination in federal government Armed forces begin to desegregate "Dixiecrat" party formed Truman defeats Dewey Kinsey report on human sexuality Transistor developed at Bell Laboratories
1949	Truman launches Fair Deal
1950	Asociación Nacional México-Americana formed
1951	J. D. Salinger, *Catcher in the Rye*
1952	Dwight D. Eisenhower elected president
1953	Submerged Lands Act

1954	*Brown* v. *Board of Education of Topeka*

1955   Montgomery bus boycott begins
        First McDonald's opens in Illinois
        AFL and CIO merge

1956   Eisenhower reelected
        Interstate Highway Act
        Allen Ginsberg, "Howl"

1957   Little Rock school integration crisis
        Civil Rights Act
        "Baby boom" peaks with 4.3 million births
        Soviet Union launches *Sputnik*

1959   One-third of all Americans reside in suburbs

1960   Three-fourths of all American families own a TV
        Civil Rights Act
        GNP hits $500 billion

Other Names to Know

William Levitt	Benjamin Spock
Betty Friedan	Jackson Pollock
Michael Harrington	Alfred Kinsey
Billy Graham	Joe Louis
Elvis Presley	Jack Kerouac

(5) GLOSSARY OF IMPORTANT TERMS

"beat generation": outsider group of young people who repudiated materialistic, conformist middle-class values in the 1950s, preferring those involving spontaneity, spirituality, intuition, and experimental lifestyles

termination policy: a policy to limit Indian self-government by eliminating reservations as legitimate political entities and settling outstanding land claims

braceros: seasonal migrant workers (helping hands) who were brought into the United States from Mexico to aid in the harvest during World War II and stayed afterward

trickle-down theory: the theory that the benefits of economic expansion would eventually trickle down to all social classes

oligopoly: the domination of industry by several firms

conglomerates: firms that diversify their holdings by buying into a variety of industries

(6) ENRICHMENT IDEAS

1. After working through the way in which clothing reflects the historical values of men and women in the decades from the 1920s to the 1960s, notice the kinds of clothes and adornments people are wearing in the 1990s. What do contemporary clothing styles say about changing values in men and women? workers? youth and older people? different racial and ethnic groups?

2. In addition to the novels cited in the chapter, you might want to read Sylvia Plath's *The Bell Jar*. In this novel, the heroine is an intelligent student at Smith College who can find no clear sense of direction. How does the plight of the main character reflect some of the themes of this chapter? J. D. Salinger's *Catcher in the Rye* is an excellent novel in which to explore a young man's anxieties and search for purpose and direction to his life, as is Ralph Ellison's *Invisible Man*.

3. An interesting exercise that can lead to insights about the past and about your own family focuses on growing up in the 1950s. You can interview one of your parents (even better both, separately) about what it was like to grow up in the decade of the 1950s. How did they spend their leisure time? What was family life like? What kind of music did they listen to? What do they now see as the most important facet of the decade for them? How well do the themes outlined in this chapter seem to fit their experiences? How was their growing up different from that of their parents? Do you see significant differences between the experiences of your mother and your father? How has your own upbringing been the same as or different from that of your parents?

4. Read some of the popular magazines of the period—*Ladies Home Journal* or *Sports Illustrated*. Study both the articles and the advertisements. What can they tell you about values and norms and about the lifestyle of middle-class Americans?

(7) SAMPLE TEST AND EXAMINATION QUESTIONS

Multiple choice: Choose the best answer.

1. All of the following describe the postwar boom EXCEPT
   a. a scarcity of consumer goods
   b. families had more discretionary income to spend
   c. enormous housing and highway construction
   d. increasing federal defense budget

2. Rising population was a result of all of the following EXCEPT
   a. rising birthrates
   b. rising marriage rates
   c. immigration
   d. falling death rates

3. Population shifted
   a. to the North
   b. to the North and Midwest
   c. to the South
   d. to the West and Southwest

4. By the end of the 1950s, what portion of Americans lived in the suburbs?
   a. one-fifth
   b. one-third
   c. one-half
   d. two-thirds

5. After 1945,
   a. antitrust activity controlled corporate growth
   b. oligopoly characterized the American economy
   c. conglomerates characterized the economy
   d. (b) and (c)

6. Despite the reaffirmation of traditional gender roles in the 1950s,
   a. many women entered the professions
   b. married women composed over half of all working women
   c. single women made up three-quarters of the female work force
   d. women began to close the income gap between women's and men's wages

7. William Levitt's houses were not
   a. pre-cut
   b. assembled quickly by a team
   c. either green, yellow, blue or pink
   d. affordable for most Americans

8. The central city declined in the 1950s as a result of movement to the suburbs by all but the
   a. middle-class
   b. department stores
   c. high-paying jobs
   d. government offices

9. In the 1950s, Americans
   a. returned to churches in large numbers
   b. had a strong working knowledge of the Bible
   c. showed extreme denominational loyalties
   d. separated religious and business values

10. The "beats"
    a. represented American mainstream culture
    b. were a black musical group
    c. were a patriotic group devoted to beating back the Russians
    d. criticized the conformity and stuffiness of the period

11. In the 1950s, the idea of working mothers was supported by
    a. Benjamin Spock
    b. Betty Friedan
    c. Alfred Kinsey
    d. Majorie Sutton

12. According to government statistics, what percentage of the population lived in poverty in 1960?
    a. 10 percent
    b. 15 percent
    c. 20 percent
    d. 25 percent

13. African-American women during this period
    a. were confined to domestic jobs
    b. stayed home with their children
    c. got white-collar jobs and increased their income
    d. entered the military

14. Operation Wetback
    a. brought braceros into the country to work for American farmers
    b. examined the terrible conditions under which migrant laborers lived and worked
    c. deported illegal immigrants and braceros who had not returned to Mexico
    d. was an effort to man the border with Mexico to prevent all illegal immigration

15. The city of the 1950s did not see the influx of
    a. African-Americans
    b. Latino-Americans
    c. Chicano-Americans
    d. Jewish-Americans

Essays

1. In the 1950s, the American dream came true for many Americans and revealed some of the limits of that dream. Discuss with evidence.

2. The rise of suburbia not only explains middle-class gender roles and patterns of consumption but also an American indifference to social problems. Discuss with relevant supporting evidence.

3. Discuss the lives and frustrations of women during this decade. What basis do you see for the women's movement?

4. If you have read *The Catcher in the Rye*, look at the character of Holden Caulfield. What does he rebel against? How successful is his rebellion? Can he stand for a certain segment of 1950s culture?

27

Chills and Fever During the Cold War

(1) CHAPTER OUTLINE

Val Lorwin, a State Department employee with 15 years of distinguished government service, is charged by an unnamed accuser of being a Communist and a security risk. After four years of struggle and new accusations, he finally clears himself of the charges before taking up a new career as a labor historian.

Origins of the Cold War
> The American Stance
> Soviet Aims
> Early Cold War Leadership
> Disillusionment with the USSR
> The Troublesome Polish Question
> Economic Pressure on the USSR
> Declaring the Cold War

Containing the Soviet Union
> Containment Defined
> The First Step: The Truman Doctrine
> The Next Steps: The Marshall Plan, NATO, and NSC-68
> Containment in the 1950s

Containment in Asia, the Middle East, and Latin America
> The Shock of the Chinese Revolution
> Stalemate in the Korean War
> Turbulence in the Middle East
> Restricting Revolt in Latin America

Atomic Weapons and the Cold War
> Sharing the Secret of the Bomb
> Nuclear Proliferation
> The Nuclear West
> "Massive Retaliation"
> Atomic Protest

The Cold War at Home
> Truman's Loyalty Program

(2) SIGNIFICANT THEMES AND HIGHLIGHTS

1. Val Lorwin's struggle reveals the central theme of this chapter: the breakdown in relations between the Soviet Union and the United States and the domestic consequences of the chills and fevers of the Cold War. Lorwin was more fortunate than many other victims of the paranoiac anti-Communist crusade and its efforts to promote ideological unity at home.

2. Aside from its ugly domestic effects—loyalty programs and the Red Scare—the Cold War thoroughly colored all foreign policy decisions of the United States from 1945 to 1990. This chapter describes Russian-American relations, the beginnings of the Cold War, and U.S. efforts to contain communism in Europe, Asia, the Middle East, and Latin America. As throughout its history, the United States was motivated by an idealistic sense of mission to make the world safe for both democracy and American capitalism.

3. When both the Soviet Union and the United States possessed nuclear weapons capable of destroying the world, a troubling and dangerous new element entered into the Cold War struggle.

4. Cold War assumptions led directly to the Vietnam War. Protestors questioned not only U.S. involvement in that particular war, but U.S. Cold War priorities as well.

(3) LEARNING GOALS

Familiarity with Basic Knowledge

After reading this chapter, you should be able to:

1. Describe the conflicting political and economic goals of the United States and the USSR for the postwar world, and how these clashing aims launched the Cold War.

2. Define containment and explain the development and meaning of the Truman Doctrine, the Marshall Plan, and NATO.

3. Outline the major events and give significance of the confrontations in Cuba under Kennedy, the war in Vietnam under Johnson and Nixon, and the improvement of relations with China and Russia under Nixon.

4. Describe the process and effects of nuclear proliferation during the Cold War.

5. Show the relationship between the Cold War and the emergence of internal loyalty programs and the second Red Scare in the United States.

Practice in Historical Thinking Skills

After reading this chapter, you should be able to:

1. Make a case for both American and Soviet responsibility for the outbreak of the Cold War.

2. Evaluate the impact of the Cold War on domestic events.

3. Assess the Cold War influence on U.S. policy in the Western Hemisphere and   Southeast Asia.

(4) IMPORTANT DATES AND NAMES TO KNOW

1945	Yalta Conference Roosevelt dies; Harry S Truman becomes president Potsdam Conference
1946	American plan for control of atomic energy fails Atomic Energy Act Iran crisis Churchill's "Iron Curtain" speech
1947	Truman Doctrine Federal Employee Loyalty Program

House Committee on Un-American Activities (HUAC) investigates the movie industry

1948
Marshall Plan launched
Berlin airlift
Israel created by United Nations
Hiss-Chambers case
Truman Elected president

1949
Soviet Union tests an atomic bomb
North Atlantic Treaty Organization (NATO) established
George Orwell publishes *1984*
Mao Zedong's forces win Chinese civil war; Jiang Jieshi flees to Taiwan

1950
Truman authorizes development of the hydrogen bomb
Alger Hiss convicted
Joseph McCarthy's Wheeling (West Virginia) speech on subversion
McCarran Internal Security Act
NSC-68

1950 - 1953
Korean War

1951
Japanese-American Treaty
Dennis v. *United States*

1952
Dwight D. Eisenhower elected president
McCarthy heads Senate Permanent Investigations Committee

1953
Stalin dies; Khrushchev consolidates power
East Germans stage anti-Soviet demonstrations
Shah of Iran returns to power in CIA-supported coup

1954
Fall of Dien Bien Phu ends French control of Indochina
Geneva Conference
Guatemalan government overthrown with CIA help
Mao's forces shell Quemoy and Matsu
Army-McCarthy hearings

1956
Suez incident
Hungarian "freedom fighters" suppressed
Eisenhower reelected

1957
Russians launch *Sputnik* satellite

1958
U.S. troops sent to support Lebanese government

1959	Castro deposes Batista in Cuba
1960	John F. Kennedy elected president
1961	Bay of Pigs invasion fails Khruschev and Kennedy meet in Vienna Berlin Wall constructed
1962	Cuban missile crisis
1963	Buddhist demonstrations in Vietnam President Diem assassinated in Vietnam Kennedy assassinated; Lyndon B. Johnson becomes president
1964	Gulf of Tonkin resolution Johnson reelected
1965	Vietnam conflict escalates Marines sent to Dominican Republic
1967-1968	Antiwar demonstrations
1968	Tet offensive in Vietnam Richard Nixon elected president My Lai incident
1969	Nixon Doctrine announced Moratorium against the Vietnam War SALT talks begin
1970	U.S.invasion of Cambodia Shootings at Kent State and Jackson State universities
1971	*New York Times* publishes Pentagon Papers
1972	Nixon visits People's Republic of China and Soviet Union Nixon reelected SALT I Treaty on nuclear arms
1973	Vietnam cease-fire agreement
1975	South Vietnam falls to the Communists; end of Vietnam War

Other Names to Know

George Marshall	Douglas MacArthur
Dean Acheson	John Foster Dulles
Ho Chi Minh	Ngo Dinh Diem
Gamal Abdel Nasser	

(5) GLOSSARY OF IMPORTANT TERMS

five-year plan: a plan devised by the Soviet state for the country's economic development

containment: the postwar policy based on the premise that the Soviet Union was an aggressive and hostile power whose further aggression around the world must be stopped by the United States

domino theory: foreign affairs belief that if one country fell to communism, adjacent countries would follow

massive retaliation: Republican policy under Dulles and Eisenhower emphasizing dependence on nuclear weapons rather than traditional arms and threatening their use

liberation: key Republican party foreign policy rhetoric under Dulles and Eisenhower, suggesting not the containment of communism but the liberation of peoples living under communism

brinkmanship: a policy related to massive retaliation in which diplomats went to the "brink" of war in the hope of deterring Soviet challenges

Viet Minh: nationalist forces in Vietnam seeking independence

Viet Cong: guerillas in South Vietnam who sought to overthrow the regime there and to install the Communist government of North Vietnam

iron curtain: a phrase introduced by Winston Churchill that suggested that the Russians had erected a barrier between the free world and the Communist world

monolithic communism: the belief that all Communist regimes were controlled by and sympathetic to the Soviet Union

coexistence: the idea that it is possible for democratic and Communist nations to exist side by side in a peaceful manner

Vietnamization: a policy of Richard Nixon whereby the United States would gradually turn over the burden of troop defense to the South Vietnamese

détente: a thawing in the Cold War, the establishment of better relations with the Soviet

Union

(6) ENRICHMENT IDEAS

1. If you had been living in the United States in 1950, how would you have voted on the questions included in public-opinion polls found in Recovering The Past for this chapter? How would you vote on the same or similar questions today? How do you explain the fact that some questions now seem out-of-date, while others are more pertinent than ever?

2. Develop a detailed chronology of foreign policy events from 1945 to 1950, showing the actions and reactions by the United States and the Soviet Union. The list should suggest the two nations' mutual responsibility for escalating tensions during the Cold War.

3. Simulate the Cold War in the game Diplomacy or Risk.

4. The Vietnam era offers another opportunity for oral history collecting. Ask family members how they felt about the war. If they were drafted, what was their experience in Vietnam? If they remained in the U.S. did they protest or support the war? Did their views of the war change over time? What events caused the change?

(7) SAMPLE TEST AND EXAMINATION QUESTIONS

Multiple choice: Choose the best answer.

1. American goals for the postwar world included
   a. eliminating trade barriers
   b. exporting vast amounts of American goods
   c. spreading democratic values
   d. all of the above

2. In 1945, the Soviets
   a. believed that they might need Germany as a buffer state
   b. expected to coexist with capitalist countries
   c. were determined to have dominance in what they saw as their sphere of interest
   d. were determined to push immediately for worldwide revolution

3. Truman and Eisenhower both
   a. believed that the United States must be tough with Russia while continuing economic aid
   b. saw the struggle with the USSR in black and white terms
   c. thought that personal diplomacy with Stalin would be effective
   d. all of the above

4. The Truman Doctrine evolved in response to
    a. the Soviet refusal to pull out of Iran
    b. trouble in Vietnam
    c. the British withdrawal from Greece and Turkey
    d. the fact that the Russians would soon develop an atomic bomb

5. The Marshall Plan provided
    a. military aid to Greece
    b. economic aid to Western Europe
    c. economic aid to Germany
    d. economic aid to Japan

6. In 1947, American policymakers favored rebuilding Germany because
    a. the country had been punished enough
    b. Hitler was dead
    c. they feared a power vacuum in central Europe
    d. they felt uncomfortable running another country

7. Americans in 1949
    a. understood the social dynamics of the Chinese Revolution
    b. recognized the links between communism and nationalism
    c. failed to understand the political and social realities of China
    d. none of the above

8. The Suez crisis led to
    a. a closing of the Suez Canal to Israeli ships
    b. an invasion by Israel, Great Britain, and France
    c. American efforts to cut off oil from their allies, Great Britain and France
    d. all of the above

9. The policy of massive retaliation proposed
    a. to fight communism anywhere by any means
    b. to retaliate against the Communists through a massive buildup of conventional weapons
    c. to use nuclear weapons to retaliate if necessary
    d. to build up the army to an unprecedented size

10. 50,000 women suspended their work one day to show their
    a. support for women's rights
    b. challenge to nuclear weapons testing
    c. contribution to the U.S. work product
    d. hatred of communism

11. The Truman loyalty program
    a. examined millions of employees and dismissed almost none
    b. examined millions of employees but dismissed only a few hundred
    c. found serious signs of Communist infiltration
    d. had so many procedural constraints that few people were ever investigated thoroughly

12. McCarthy's hold over American life was strengthened by
    a. his use of the press and television
    b. the accuracy of his accusations
    c. the support he received from Eisenhower
    d. his sympathetic character

13. U.S. involvement in Vietnam
    a. was promoted by the commitment to stop the spread of communism
    b. escalated dramatically in 1965 under Johnson
    c. was a gradual process that took place over several administrations
    d. all of the above

14. Vietnam protestors
    a. were mostly educated students from elite colleges
    b. challenged many assumptions of the Cold War
    c. found polite "teach-ins" to be their most effective tools
    d. never reached significant numbers

15. The Pentagon Papers
    a. revealed the faulty assumptions and fabrications that led to the Vietnam situation
    b. revealed the guilt of Alger Hiss
    c. outlined the Nixon Doctrine
    d. were published by the Nixon White House

Matching: Match the person or place in the left column with the most appropriate term in the right column.

_____1. George Kennan   a. brinkmanship
_____2. Joseph McCarthy   b. Truman Doctrine
_____3. Guatemala   c. liberation
_____4. Hungary   d. containment
_____5. Cuban missile crisis   e. iron curtain
_____6. Winston Churchill   f. internal security
_____7. Greece and Turkey   g. Viet Minh
_____8. Dien Bien Phu   h. CIA

Essays

1. Make a case for both American and Soviet responsibility for the outbreak of the Cold War.

2. "The most profound effects of the Cold War were on domestic life, not foreign relations." Discuss.

3. Trace the background and major crisis points of the Cold War.

4. Discuss the U.S. policy toward Cuba during the Eisenhower and the Kennedy administrations. What were the U.S.'s motivations in dealing with this neighbor? How might the situation have been improved?

5. Trace U.S. involvement in Vietnam. Discuss the Vietnam War as a Cold War event.

Identify and Interpret: Quotation
(that is, state who, what, where, when, and why significant)

Local defense will always be important. But there is no local defense which alone will contain the mighty land power of the Communist world. Local defenses must be reinforced by the further deterrent of massive retaliatory power. A potential aggressor must know that he cannot always prescribe battle conditions that suit him. Otherwise, for example, a potential aggressor, who is glutted with manpower, might be tempted to attack in confidence that resistance would be confined to manpower. He might be tempted to attack in places where his superiority was decisive. The way to deter aggression is for the free community to be willing and able to respond vigorously at places and with means of its own choosing.

Identify and Interpret: Chart

(that is, first, study the chart and describe what it shows; second, analyze the chart by explaining some of the reasons behind the patterns you see; third, assess the larger significance of the chart)

Map Question: locate the following on the accompanying map.

1. Korea
2. China
3. Formosa (Taiwan)
4. Iran
5. Dien Bien Phu
6. Suez Canal
7. Yalta
8. Spain

9. Hungary
10. Poland
11. Berlin
12. Normandy
13. Greece and Turkey
14. Lebanon
15. India
16. Vietnam

28

High Water and Ebb Tide of the Liberal State

(1) CHAPTER OUTLINE

Paul Cowan was a child of privilege who, like many Americans in the 1960s, felt that he should give something back to the less fortunate. After an elite education at Choate and Harvard, Cowan worked in the civil rights movement in Mississippi, then volunteered with the Peace Corps in Ecuador. His experiences in South America caused him to question the true motives behind his liberal agenda. Along with many other Americans, Cowan moved from enthusiastic liberalism to more tempered conservatism in the 1970s.

The Origins of the Welfare State
    Truman's Approach
    Truman's Struggle with a Conservative Congress
    The Fair Deal and Its Fate
    The Election of Eisenhower
    "Modern Republicanism"

The High Water Mark of Liberalism
    The Election of 1960
    The New Frontier
    The Change of Command
    The Great Society in Action
    A Sympathetic Supreme Court
    The Great Society Under Attack

The Decline of Liberalism
    The Election of 1968
    The Republican Agenda
    The Watergate Affair
    Gerald Ford: Caretaker President
    The Carter Interlude

Conclusion: Political Readjustment

(2) SIGNIFICANT THEMES AND HIGHLIGHTS

1. Paul Cowan's individual odyssey from committed liberal activism to disillusioned conservatism mirrors the course of American politics during the 1960s and 1970s. Building on the foundation begun by FDR and continued under Truman and Eisenhower, the 1960s marked the height of optimistic hopes that the government could solve the nation's domestic problems. The liberal agenda of the 1960s under John Kennedy and Johnson was replaced by pessimism, doubts, and uncertainty under Republican leadership and the Carter presidency in the 1970s. The morality of government as well as its ineffectual role was questioned as a result of the Vietnam War, the Watergate crisis, and the decline of the liberal state.

2. The domestic programs of the 1940s and 1950s under Truman and Eisenhower and the liberal welfare assumptions of John Kennedy's New Frontier and Lyndon Johnson's Great Society represented a major assault on serious social and economic problems. That they fell far short of their goals raised questions in subsequent Republican administrations over how far government should or would go in providing for the welfare of its citizens.

(3) LEARNING GOALS

Familiarity with Basic Knowledge

After reading this chapter, you should be able to:

1. Detail the rise of the welfare state during the administrations of Truman and Eisenhower.

2. Define the meaning of John Kennedy's "New Frontier" and describe the tone, achievements, and failures of his administration.

3. Define Lyndon Johnson's "Great Society" and describe how well it achieved or failed to achieve its goals.

4. Describe the goals and style of leadership under the Republican administrations of Richard Nixon and Gerald Ford.

5. Tell the story of the presidential elections of 1952, 1960, 1968, 1972, and 1976, including the story of Watergate.

6. Identify the arguments for and against strong assertions of governmental power in the 1960s and 1970s.

Practice in Historical Thinking Skills

After reading this chapter, you should be able to:

1. Explain and analyze the strengths and weaknesses of the liberal state in the 1960s and 1970s.

2. Analyze the goals, styles, achievements, and limitations of the presidential administrations of Truman, Eisenhower, Kennedy, Johnson, Nixon, Ford, and Carter.

3. Explain and defend, with historical examples, your own position on the proper role of the federal government in domestic affairs in this changing world.

(4) IMPORTANT DATES AND NAMES TO KNOW

1946	Employment Act
1947	Taft-Hartley Act
1948	"Dixiecrat" party formed Truman defeats Dewey
1949	Truman launches Fair Deal
1952	Dwight D. Eisenhower elected president
1953	Submerged Lands Act
1956	Eisenhower reelected
1960	John F. Kennedy elected president
1962	JFK confronts steel companies
1963	Kennedy assassinated; Lyndon B. Johnson becomes president
1964	Economic Opportunity Act initiates War on Poverty Johnson reelected
1965	Department of Housing and Urban Development established Elementary and Secondary Education Act
1968	Robert F. Kennedy assassinated Police and protestors clash at Democratic national convention Richard M. Nixon elected president

1972	Nixon reelected
1973	Watergate hearings in Congress Spiro Agnew resigns as vice-president
1974	OPEC price increases Inflation hits 11 percent Unemployment reaches 7.1 percent Nixon resigns; Gerald R. Ford becomes president Ford pardons Nixon
1975	Unemployment reaches 12 percent
1976	Jimmy Carter elected president
1977	Carter energy program

Other Names to Know

Adlai Stevenson	George Humphrey
Hubert Humphrey	Eugene McCarthy
Lee Harvey Oswald	Barry Goldwater
George Wallace	Mayor Richard Daley
Warren Burger	Spiro Agnew
Henry Kissinger	Daniel Ellsberg
H. R. Haldeman	John Ehrlichman
John Mitchell	G. Gordon Liddy
Charles E. Wilson	Strom Thurmond
Rachel Carson	Bob Woodward
Carl Bernstein	Daniel Patrick Moynihan

(5) GLOSSARY OF IMPORTANT TERMS

Fair Deal: Truman's liberal domestic agenda which raised the minimum wage, instituted farming and housing programs, and desegregated the military.

Dixiecrats: states' rights party that opposed the Democratic party's move towards civil rights for African-Americans.

Peace Corps: program established by Kennedy which sent volunteer Americans abroad to assist developing countries

Job Corps: program established by Johnson to provide training for unskilled young people

VISTA: Johnson's program in which volunteers addressed problems in America

(6) ENRICHMENT IDEAS

1. Recovering The Past suggests the power of television to shape American views and responses to events. Television also conveyed the norms of the period and captured some of the confusion and anger that changing values and tastes could generate. You may be able to see some reruns of programs from the 1960s; if so, look for evidence of social values, for suggestions of gender and age norms, for signs of challenges to familiar ways of thought and action, and even for typical prime-time programming that shows another side to the 1960s than protest.

2. Interview people about their recollections of and reactions to Watergate, the Nixon administration, and the change in social mood from the intense public activism of the 1960s to the inward-looking privatism of the 1970s. Would they agree with that description? If not, how do they explain it?

(7) SAMPLE TEST AND EXAMINATION QUESTIONS

1. The Employment Act of 1946
   a. committed the government to maintaining full employment
   b. was designed to stave off another depression
   c. was watered down by Congress because of the fears of the business community
   d. all of the above

2. The Taft-Hartley Act
   a. extended the powers given to labor by the Wagner Act
   b. won Truman's support
   c. limited the power of unions
   d. was a banking bill

3. Eisenhower
   a. hoped to turn back the clock and revive the Republicanism of the 1920s
   b. as a former general had no defined governmental philosophy
   c. espoused dynamic conservatism
   d. wanted to increase governmental spending if that would ensure Republican dominance

4. Kennedy won the 1960 election because
   a. he did well with black and ethnic voters
   b. he projected an effective image during the TV debates
   c. he was able to defuse the issue of his Catholicism
   d. all of the above

5. JFK, LBJ, and RMN believed
   a. that American society was fundamentally flawed
   b. that goods needed to be more widely shared

c. that the poor need only to work hard to succeed

d. that slogans could conceal the fact that nothing would be done about social problems

6. All of Kennedy's efforts on the domestic front failed EXCEPT

   a. efforts to cut corporate taxes

   b. grants to states for school aid

   c. securing funds for the space program

   d. a strong civil rights bill

7. LBJ pressed for

   a. a poverty bill

   b. Medicare

   c. aid to elementary and secondary schools

   d. all of the above

8. Radicals criticized the Great Society programs because

   a. the poor did not have a broad enough vision of American needs

   b. there was no real effort to redistribute income

   c. authority was too centralized

   d. all of the above

9. The Great Society suffered the final blow from

   a. the Dixiecrats

   b. the effort to maintain war in Vietnam

   c. the environmental movement

   d. radical moves to expand programs

10. When the Arab oil embargo ended in 1974,

    a. prices jumped due to double-digit inflation

    b. prices began a downward drop halted only with the election of Ronald Reagan

    c. unemployment reached a new high of 5 percent

    d. unemployment dropped as prices rose to new highs

11. Nixon's Family Assistance Plan

    a. was criticized by liberals as socialistic

    b. guaranteed a minimum annual income to poor families

    c. was changed so badly by the Senate that he vetoed it

    d. required participants to serve two years in the armed forces in order to support their families

12. Nixon's campaign for law and order was led by his attorney general,

    a. Spiro Agnew

    b. H. R. Haldeman

    c. John Mitchell

    d. John Dean

13. The Supreme Court under Chief Justice Burger
    a. tilted to the right
    b. guaranteed a woman's right to choose abortion
    c. upheld community standards on pornography
    (d.) all of the above

14. In the Watergate affair, President Nixon was
    a. guilty only of bad judgment, not of any wrong-doing
    b. impeached by the House of Representatives for his refusal to turn over the White House tapes
    c. impeached on four counts by the House, but the Senate failed to convict him
    (d.) able to resign before the House voted on impeachment

15. Jimmy Carter
    a. had a good working relationship with Congress
    b. surrounded himself with brilliant advisors and Washington insiders
    (c.) was an uncomfortable technocrat
    d. all of the above

Essays

1. Compare and contrast the presidential goals, styles, accomplishments, and limitations of John F. Kennedy and Lyndon B. Johnson.

2. Explain and defend with historical examples your own position on the proper role of the federal government in domestic affairs.

3. Describe Richard Nixon's aims, accomplishments, and failures as president. What is his legacy?

THE COMPUTER

In the late twentieth century, the computer is practically synonymous with technology. *Computer* originally meant a person or thing that could count or calculate with numbers, but the word's Latin root means "to think." To think, of course, is to process information, whether it concerns money, distance, temperature, or time. The ability to process, store, and use information distinguishes the modern computer from early calculating devices like the abacus.

Twentieth-century advances in the fields of electrical engineering and solid-state physics as well as in formal logic, propositional calculus, and information theory made possible the development of a machine that could do more than count. War made such a machine highly desirable. The military requirements of World War II— including the engineering of the atomic bomb—promoted research on and development of what came to be known as the computer. British scientists developed a machine to help break codes, while the U.S. Army established a ballistics research laboratory at the University of Pennsylvania. By 1943, mathematicians and engineers at Penn were working on the first all-electronic general-purpose computer, named ENIAC. Despite its ability to perform 5,000 additions or 300 multiplications in a second, ENIAC had significant limitations. It had almost no memory and could not store programs. Its huge size (80 feet long and 8 feet high) and complex construction (18,000 vacuum tubes) also caused problems.

After the war, commercial efforts to improve computers got under way. The U.S. Census Bureau was the first customer for the UNIVAC, the earliest commercially developed system. CBS used its UNIVAC to predict the results of the 1952 election. Rapid improvement was spurred by several developments by American scientists: the transistor in 1948, the integrated circuit in the 1960s, and the microprocessor, the "computer on a chip," in 1971.

No short account of computers can begin to suggest the range of their capabilities and the impact they have had on our lives. Computers navigate spacecraft, route telephone calls, record financial trades, diagnose diseases—and design new computers. The largest machines, called supercomputers, are used to simulate aircraft behavior, forecast weather, and do exotic scientific research. They cost millions of dollars each, are made by only a handful of manufacturers in the world, take up a good-size room, and perform hundreds of millions of operations a second. The smallest machines, called application-specific integrated circuits (ASICs), control the engines, weapons, or bodily organs in which they are embedded. They are no bigger than a small cookie and cost less than $1,000 each. In between are office mainframes, minis, workstations, micros, and a range of home computers. Perhaps the most readily understood marvel of the computer revolution is that in a typical recent year in one category of microcomputer alone (the $2,000 desktop machine), 3 million units were placed in service. Each was more sophisticated, more powerful, and more reliable that ENIAC.

In their impact on the physical environment, computers are fundamentally different from other technologies of the twentieth century. Electric power generation, the internal combustion engine, and new chemicals have put tremendous stresses, directly and indirectly, on the earth. The computer has the potential of dealing with these stresses; it can reduce the need to travel, make machinery more energy-efficient, and monitor pollution. In the human arena, the computer is already taking us into two contradictory directions. On the one hand, it enhances centralization by increasing the power of large organizations; on the other hand, its contributions to individual freedom and discretion encourage decentralization. Arguments can be made to support either tendency. Perhaps both will remain equally strong, producing a world in which individuals and organizations learn to respect each other more than they have in the past.

29

The Struggle for Social Reform

(1) CHAPTER OUTLINE

Ann Clarke, born Antonina Rose Rumore, put her Lower East Side, New York City, Italian working-class origins behind her as she went to California and married a college-educated chemist. After 15 years of faithful devotion to her husband and three children, she enrolled in college. Not without considerable conflict and worries, especially over her "sixties"-style children, Ann managed to complete a degree and start a career of her own as a teacher.

The Black Struggle for Equality
    Mid-Twentieth-Century Roots
    Integrating the Schools
    Black Gains on Other Fronts
    Confrontation Continues
    Kennedy's Response
    Legislative Success in the Johnson Years
    Black Power Challenges Liberal Reform
    "Southern Strategy" and Showdown on Civil Rights

Pressure from the Women's Movement
    Attacking the Feminine Mystique
    Feminism at High Tide

Latino Mobilization
    Early Efforts for Equality
    César Chávez and the Politics of Confrontation

Native American Protest
    Origins of the Struggle
    Tribal Voices
    Confrontational Tactics
    Government Response

Social and Cultural Protest
    Student Activism
    The Counterculture
    Gay and Lesbian Rights

Conclusion: Extending the American Dream

(2) SIGNIFICANT THEMES AND HIGHLIGHTS

1. The changes Ann Clarke went through typified those of millions of other women in the 1960s and 1970s. Traumatic alterations in traditional patterns of women's experience and family life grew out of and compounded the struggle for social reform that has marked American life since the 1960s, the third reform cycle in the Twentieth century.

2. The dominant reform movement of the era was the black struggle for equality. This chapter traces that struggle from the civil rights movements of the early sixties under Martin Luther King, Jr., to the black power movement of the late sixties inspired by the martyred Malcolm X, and finally to the lessening of concern among white Americans for black equality and rights in the Republican presidential administrations of the 1970s and 1980s.

3. In the continuing effort to fulfill the American dream for all people, blacks, women, and Native Americans were joined by Vietnam veterans, Latinos, and advocates for gay and lesbian liberation in an effort to improve the quality of life for all Americans.

4. Resistance to these movements by the established order and older generation, along with the escalating war in Vietnam, fed both the idealism and disillusionment of young people, who embraced political radicalism and adopted new standards of cultural taste and personal behavior.

(3) LEARNING GOALS

Familiarity with Basic Knowledge

After reading this chapter, you should be able to:

1. Describe the major confrontations over civil rights in the 1960s, and compare and contrast Kennedy's and Johnson's responses to the black struggle for equality with the policies of Republican presidencies from Nixon to Bush.

2. Explain the reasons for the shift in the civil rights movement from its nonviolent phase to the black power militancy of the late sixties.

3. State the major goals of feminist leaders and show the similarities between the women's and civil rights movements.

4. Describe the efforts of Hispanic (Latino) and Native American leaders and groups to improve their position and quality of life, and show how these movements also were patterned on the black experience.

5. Explain the reasons for the student protest movement and characterize the values of the counterculture.

6. Describe the environmental and consumer protection movements.

Practice in Historical Thinking Skills

After reading this chapter, you should be able to:

1. Analyze and evaluate the reasons for the shift in the black struggle from nonviolent direct action to black power.

2. Explain how and why governmental support for civil rights in the 1960s, however tentative, deteriorated in the 1970s and 1980s.

3. Discuss the influence of the black movement for equality and rights on those by women, Latinos, Native Americans, and gays.

4. Describe and evaluate the influence of youth culture in recent American life.

(4) IMPORTANT DATES AND NAMES TO KNOW

1947	Jackie Robinson breaks the color line in major league baseball
1950	Asociación Nacional México-Americana formed
1954	*Brown* v. *Board of Education*
1955	Montgomery, Alabama, bus boycott begins
1957	Little Rock, Arkansas, school integration crisis Civil Rights Act
1960	Civil Rights Act Birth control pill becomes available Sit-ins begin Students for a Democratic Society (SDS) founded
1961	Freedom rides Joseph Heller, *Catch-22;* Ken Kesey, *One Flew Over the Cuckoo's Nest*

1962	James Meredith crisis at the University of Mississippi SDS's Port Huron Statement Rachel Carson, *Silent Spring*
1963	Birmingham demonstration Civil rights March on Washington Betty Friedan, *The Feminine Mystique*
1964	Civil Rights Act Free speech movement, Berkeley
1965	Martin Luther King, Jr., leads march from Selma to Montgomery Voting Rights Act United Farm Workers grape strike Malcolm X assassinated Riots in Watts section of Los Angeles Ralph Nader, *Unsafe at Any Speed*
1966	Stokely Carmichael becomes head of SNCC and calls for "black power" Black Panthers founded NOW founded Masters and Johnson, *Human Sexual Response*
1967	Urban riots in 22 cities
1968	Martin Luther King, Jr., assassinated Student demonstrations at Columbia and elsewhere Chicano student walkouts American Indian Movement (AIM) founded
1969	Woodstock and Altamont rock festivals Weathermen's "Days of Rage" in Chicago Native Americans seize Alcatraz La Raza Unida founded
1971 - 1975	School busing controversies in North and South
1972	*Ms.* magazine founded Congress passes Equal Rights Amendment
1973	AIM occupies Wounded Knee, South Dakota
1975	Farmworkers' grape boycott Indian Self-determination and Education Assistance Acts
1978	*Bakke* v. *Regents of the University of California*

1979	Accident at Three Mile Island nuclear power plant
1982	Ratification of ERA fails

Other Names to Know

Anne Moody	Gloria Steinem
"Bull" Connor	Tom Hayden
James Meredith	Mario Savio
César Chávez	Phyllis Schlafly
James Baldwin	Reis López Tijerina
José Angel Gutiérrez	Jesse Jackson
Bob Dylan	Toney Anaya
Henry Cisneros	Huey Newton
Medgar Evers	Rosa Parks
Sufi Abdul Hamid	Marabel Morgan
Fannie Lou Hamer	

(5) GLOSSARY OF IMPORTANT TERMS

New Left: term referring to the liberals and radicals in the 1960s who, unlike the old Communist left of the 1930s, were more interested in such issues as civil rights, poverty, and militarism than in industrial issues like better wages and hours and the rights of collective bargaining; also believed in a leadership style of participatory democracy rather than reliance on party doctrine

"Me Decade:" label for the 1970s referring to the various movements, in the frustrating aftermath of the 1960s, that looked inward at one's personal relationships and growth rather than outward at social changes

(6) ENRICHMENT IDEAS

1. After working through the songs and questions in Recovering The Past for this chapter, find popular songs from the 1970s and 1980s and analyze how they reflect the values, priorities, and concerns of the American people in those decades. Examine song lyrics as if they were poems. What is the representative music of the age now, and what does it say about how "the times they are [still] a-changin'"? How have the values among young people changed in the past 40 years?

2. There are so many possibilities for enriching the study of the 1960s that only a few need be suggested here: feature films (*The Graduate, Dr. Strangelove, Bonnie and Clyde, Easy Rider,* etc.); novels (Joseph Heller, *Catch-22;* Ken Kesey, *One Flew over the Cuckoo's Nest;* Peter Tauber, *The Last Best Hope;* N. Scott Momaday, *House Made of Dawn;*

Marge Piercy, *Small Changes,* etc.); rock and folk music (the Beatles; the Rolling Stones; Peter, Paul and Mary, etc.). Your imagination can come into full play in researching and reliving this recent and memorable decade.

3. As you approach the present, issues of interpretation (or lack of interpretation) become more pressing and controversial. Some historians argue that interpreting the recent past is impossible and should be avoided, while others insist that providing an interpretive understanding of contemporary history is a crucial responsibility. To what extent does this chapter have an interpretation? Does it correspond to your view or that of your parents?

(7) SAMPLE TEST AND EXAMINATION QUESTIONS

Multiple choice: Choose the best answer.

1. Which of the following black organizations was the most militant in carrying the struggle for civil rights into direct action and inflammatory rhetoric?
   a. SCLC
   b. SNCC
   c. NAACP
   d. CORE

2. Kennedy moved slowly on civil rights because
   a. he was not interested in the plight of blacks
   b. he thought that his attack on racial segregation in federally funded housing was a strong enough statement on civil rights
   c. he thought that since blacks had not voted for him in 1960, it was not politically important for him to heed them
   d. he needed southern votes in Congress on other issues

3. The black power movement emerged for all of the following reasons EXCEPT
   a. disillusionment with the Democratic party over treatment of the Mississippi Freedom Democrats at the national convention
   b. the slow pace of change despite years of struggle
   c. the influence of Malcolm X and Stokely Carmichael
   d. Dr. King's repudiation of nonviolence

4. The *Bakke* decision stated that
   a. race could no longer be considered in school admissions policies
   b. racial quotas could not be used
   c. racial quotas were justified
   d. reverse discrimination was entirely justified

5. In the 1980s, all of the following statistics were true, EXCEPT
    a. the ratio of median black-to-white family income did not change
    b. the percentage of blacks enrolled in college decreased slightly
    c. the ratio of black-to-white female earnings decreased from 1970s levels
    d. special black training programs lowered black unemployment rates

6. All of these areas reflected an erosion of white support for civil rights in the 1970s and 1980s, EXCEPT
    a. enforcement of busing and school desegregation
    b. the election of black political candidates
    c. affirmative action attitudes and government policies
    d. the condition of blacks in urban areas

7. In the 1980s, women
    a. finally earned equal wages for doing the same work as men
    b. remained mostly in traditional women's jobs
    c. did not often work if they were married with young children
    d. finally moved into more and more top management and political offices

8. The goals of the women's movement in the 1970s included all of the following EXCEPT
    a. equal employment opportunities
    b. the Equal Rights Amendment
    c. the legalization of lesbian marriages
    d. child-care centers and abortion reform

9. One of the major achievements of the struggle by Hispanic-Americans was
    a. the standoff against federal marshals at Wounded Knee
    b. the winning of support from President Nixon
    c. the removal of all immigration restrictions against Mexicans
    d. a growing presence in education and in local and national politics since the 1960s

10. César Chávez and the United Farm Workers
    a. rejected traditional union strategies for political organization
    b. urged immigrant workers to return to Mexico
    c. launched successful boycotts of lettuce and grape growers in California
    d. were denied the right to bargain collectively by the National Labor Relations Board

11. The American Indian Movement was an organization that initially
    a. tried to help urban Indians
    b. tried to help Indians on the reservations
    c. sued the central government for violated treaty rights
    d. focused on regaining land, water, and fishing rights

12. The most important factor contributing to the social changes of the 1960s was
    a. the coming of age of the baby-boom generation
    b. radicalism among women
    c. rock music
    d. the use of drugs

13. The student movement was fueled primarily by
    a. charismatic leadership
    b. the Vietnam conflict
    c. sympathetic college administrations
    d. support from the working class

14. Environmentalists have been primarily concerned since the 1960s about all of the following EXCEPT
    a. saving sharks and porpoises
    b. oil spills
    c. nuclear power plants
    d. chemical pesticides

15. Eisenhower sent federal troops to Little Rock because
    a. he energetically pursued a civil rights policy
    b. Governor Orval Faubus was a political threat
    c. he could not tolerate resistance to the law
    d. he was eager to remind black voters of the historical connections between blacks and the Republican party

Matching: Match the names in the left column with the most appropriate term from the right column.

____1. Mississippi Freedom Democratic party	a. black power
____2. Jose Angel Gutiérrez	b. Wounded Knee
____3. Gloria Steinem	c. University of Mississippi
____4. Betty Friedan	d. Earth Day
____5. César Chávez	e. *Ms.*
____6. Tom Hayden	f. La Raza Unida
____7. James Meredith	g. SDS Port Huron Statement
____8. AIM	h. NOW
____9. Rachel Carson	i. United Farm Workers' movement
___10. Stokely Carmichael	j. 1964 Democratic national convention

Essays

1. Analyze and evaluate the reasons for and wisdom of the shift in the black struggle from nonviolent direct action to black power.

2. Compare and contrast the goals, tactics, and problems of the movements by blacks, women, Hispanics, and Native Americans, indicating which you think was most successful and why.

3. Describe and evaluate the student movement and the counterculture in the 1960s and 1970s. Do you think young protesters made more of an impact politically or culturally? on events or on lifestyle?

4. Select one film, one novel, and one song or musical group, showing how each reflected the mood, values, and social concerns of each of the decades: the 1960s, the 1970s, and the 1980s.

Identify and Interpret: Quotation
(that is, state who, what, where, when, and why significant)

You may well ask: 'Why direct action? Why sit-ins, marches and so forth? Isn't negotiation a better path?' You are quite right in calling for negotiation. Indeed, this is the very purpose of direct action. Nonviolent direct action seeks to create such a crisis and foster such a tension that a community which has constantly refused to negotiate is forced to confront the issue. It seeks so to dramatize the issue that it can no longer be ignored.

For many of us it was the very first time we had joined together with other women to talk and think about our lives and what we could do about them. . . . Finding out about our bodies and our bodies' needs, starting to take control over that area of our lives, has released for us an energy that has overflowed into our work, our friendships, our relationships with men and women, and for some of us, our marriage and our parenthood. . . . Our image of ourselves is on a firmer base, we can be better friends and better lovers, better people, more self-confident, more autonomous, stronger and more whole.

30

The Revival of Conservatism

(1) CHAPTER OUTLINE

Until the early 1990s, TWA paid Craig Miller $15.65 an hour as a sheet metal worker. Miller provided a comfortable middle-class lifestyle for his family. However, downturns in the economy forced many industries, including airlines, to lay off workers like Miller. He and his wife patched together a living from various low-skilled service sector jobs. Their plight illustrates the growing gap between rich and poor and the country's shift towards a service economy. The Millers' refusal to apply for the food stamps their reduced income demanded highlights the debate over the appropriate role government should play in the lives of its citizens.

The Conservative Transformation
> The New Politics
> Conservative Leadership
> Republican Policies at Home
> Liberal Interlude
> Conservative Resurgence

An End to Social Reform
> Slowdown in the Struggle for Civil Rights
> Obstacles to Women's Rights
> The Limited Commitment to Latino Rights
> Continuing Problems for Native Americans
> Pressures on the Environmental Movement

The Post-Industrial Economy
> The Changing Nature of Work
> The Shift to a Service Economy
> Workers in Transition
> The Roller Coaster Economy

Demographic and Regional Change
> Urban and Suburban Shifts
> Western Development
> The New Pilgrims
> Growing Up

Growing Old
Growing Poor

The United States in a Changed World
Triumph in the Cold War
Steps Toward Peace in the Middle East
Turbulence in Latin America
Upheaval in Africa

Conclusion: The Recent Past in Perspective

(2) SIGNIFICANT THEMES AND HIGHLIGHTS

1. The dominant theme of this latest chapter in American history is that of a disordered economy under the conservative leadership of Presidents Reagan and Bush in the 16 years from 1981 to 1997.. America's economic woes in the eighties severely affected the lives of industrial workers like Craig Miller, as well as of mid-level corporate executives, middle-class families, people of color who have known poverty for years, and women heading single-parent families.

2. A demographic transformation of enormous proportions gave American society an increasingly varied color in the 1980s and 1990s. Immigrants from Latin America and the Far East introduced new pilgrims into the mosaic of the American people, causing a crisis of identity for the multicultural, polylingual American society. Americans were older, more often divorced, and more often living in nontraditional households.

3. With the tearing down of the Berlin Wall and the collapse of the former Soviet Union and its Eastern European allies in the dramatic events of 1989, the Cold War ended. With a vastly changed world order, Americans faced a new role in their foreign relationship not only with Europe and Russia but with countries in Asia, the Middle East, Latin America, and Africa.

4. As Bill Clinton assumed the presidency in 1993, he faced domestic challenges as well. His administration and, after the 1994 elections, the Republican-controlled Congress, placed new limits on the federal government as they helped the American people fulfill old and new dreams as the century neared its end.

(3) LEARNING GOALS

Familiarity with Basic Knowledge

After reading this chapter, you should be able to:

1. Show how the conservative policies of the Reagan and Bush presidencies contributed to the disordered and declining economy of the 1980s.

2. Identify four important recent demographic changes in American society and explain the consequences each is having on our lives as Americans.

3. Describe the American role in the rapidly changing world of Asia, Africa, Latin America, the Middle East, Europe, and the countries of the former Soviet Union.

Practice in Historical Thinking Skills

After reading this chapter, you should be able to:

1. Understand how America's role in the world has dramatically changed, and the extent to which old principles and practices of foreign policy might still guide America's relationship with the rest of an increasingly smaller world.

2. Evaluate the ways in which the conservative administrations of Reagan and Bush represented a shift away from the liberal domestic policies of the country since the New Deal, and how effective they were in meeting the economic, political, and social needs of the American people.

3. Identify and analyze the enduring continuities and tensions in the American people that persist in our lives today.

(4) IMPORTANT DATES AND NAMES TO KNOW

1980	Ronald Reagan elected president
1980 - 1982	Recession
1981	Reagan breaks air controllers' strike AIDS (acquired immune deficiency syndrome) discovered
1981 - 1983	Tax cuts; deficit spending increases
1982	U.S. invasion of Lebanon
1983	Reagan proposes Strategic Defense Initiative ("Star Wars")
1984	Reagan reelected
1986	Immigration Reform and Control Act

Tax reform measure passed

1987   Iran-*contra* affair becomes public
          Stock market crashes
          Intermediate-Range Nuclear Forces Treaty signed

1988   George Bush elected president

1989   Federal bailout of savings and loan industry
          Fall of the Berlin Wall

1990   National debt reaches $3.1 trillion
          Immigration Act of 1990
          Sandinistas driven from power in Nicaragua
          Nelson Mandela freed in South Africa
          U.S. population is 250 million

1990 - 1992   Recession

1991   Persian Gulf War
          Failed coup in Soviet Union
          Disintegration of the Soviet Union
          Strategic Arms Reduction Treaty (START) signed

1991-1996   Ethnic turbulence in fragmented former Yugoslavia

1992   Bill Clinton elected president
          Czechoslovakia splits into separate Czech and Slovak Republics
          Riots erupt in Los Angeles

1993   North American Free Trade Agreement (NAFTA) ratified
          Palestine Liberation Organization and Israel sign peace treaty

1994   Nelson Mandela elected president of South Africa

Other Names to Know

James Baker	Daniel Ortega
Jerry Falwell	Anwar el-Sadat
Menachem Begin	General Alexander Haig
Ayatollah Khomeini	Walter Mondale
Lech Walesa	Saddam Hussein

(5) GLOSSARY OF IMPORTANT TERMS

Moral Majority: a conservative pressure group, relying on modern communications and fund-raising techniques, which sought to reestablish what it defined as "traditional values" (dissolved in 1989)

perestroika: restructuring the Russian economy

glasnost: political openness to encourage personal initiative

supply-side economics ("Reaganomics"): the view that tax reductions will encourage business investment and expansion, which will in turn generate general economic growth and prosperity

(6) ENRICHMENT IDEAS

1. Autobiographies—your own as well as those by Franklin, Stanton, Malcolm X, and others—reveal the story of the American people. An autobiography, as Thoreau's *Walden* suggests, need not, in fact, cannot "cover" one's entire life. Like historians, autobiographers face problems of sources, selection, embellishment, and interpretation. The following short exercise will reveal these problems, as well as some insights into yourself.

    First, research and write (in two pages) the story of your life for a month's time three years ago. This will no doubt raise problems primarily of sources—how to find out what you were doing, what happened during that month. Writing about your life will also raise issues of embellishment as you seek to describe and maybe even to interpret those half-remembered high school horrors. Second, research and write (in two pages) the story of your life last week. Note that your primary problem here is not memory and sources but selection. How will you decide which among the hundreds of facts you know about your life last week should be selected? Perhaps an interpretive framework, a theme, or a thesis point of view will help.

    Conclude your autobiography with one paragraph that connects or shows the relationship between the you of three years ago and the you of last week. The connecting theme might be found in a significant continuity, in a change, or in something else, but whatever it is, it will suggest the importance of interpretation in transforming a catalog of factual events into a story. In writing this paper about your own life, you are, in the highest sense, doing history.

2. This chapter covers the recent past, which is accessible to you in a way that other periods are not. You might want to think about the way in which the chapter treats these years. Would you characterize them in the same way? What would you consider to be the greatest problems of the recent past? The most positive features? How have the currents of recent years affected your family and your own hopes and dreams?

(7) SAMPLE TEST AND EXAMINATION QUESTIONS

Multiple choice: Choose the best answer.

1. Craig Miller's story represents
    a. the economic success of the triumph of conservatism under President Reagan
    b. the increasingly competitive nature of white-collar executive positions in the 1980s
    c. the corporate down-sizing that accompanied an extended recession
    d. a personal tragedy of the end of the Cold War

2. The conservative coalition in the new politics of the 1980s included
    a. advocates of free market economic policies
    b. religious fundamentalists
    c. middle-class voters who felt threatened by gains of the poor and minorities
    d. all of the above

3. Republican policies in domestic affairs focused on
    a. tax cuts, especially for the wealthier classes
    b. tighter regulation of industry and labor
    c. vigorous protection of the environment
    d. all of the above

4. The "New Federalism"
    a. turned civil rights regulation over to the states
    b. forced many states and municipalities nearly into bankruptcy
    c. cut the national debt by millions of dollars
    d. let states decide whether or not to permit abortion

5. In the 1980s
    a. the share of national wealth by the wealthiest 1 percent of the nation doubled
    b. the net worth of the wealthiest 1 percent of Americans declined
    c. the gap between rich and poor narrowed
    d. women and minorities continued to gain economically compared to white males

6. The American economy in the 1980s
    a. slowed its productivity in the industrial sector
    b. shifted to the service sector
    c. was challenged by industrial growth in other parts of the world
    d. all of the above

7. Clinton's cabinet and the 1992 Congress
    a. included more minorities and women than ever before
    b. refused to ratify NAFTA

   c. strongly supported health care reform

   d. all of the above

8. The Contract With America
   a. scale back the role of the federal government
   b. balance the budget
   c. reduce taxes
   d. all of the above

9. Pink-collar positions
   a. paid as much as men's traditional jobs
   b. were mostly eliminated in the 1980s
   c. continued to be held by women in the 80s and 90s
   d. were mostly above the corporate "glass ceiling"

10. The use of computers in the workplace helped
    a. workers connect more strongly to their jobs
    b. increase productivity
    c. decrease the average number of hours in the work week
    d. decrease physical and emotional stress in the workplace

11. The Stock Market Crash of 1987 was caused by
    a. federal budget deficit
    b. negative trade balances
    c. exposures of Wall Street fraud
    d. all of the above

12. The largest group of immigrant "New Pilgrims" came from
    a. Mexico, the Caribbean, and Latin America
    b. Europe and Canada
    c. China, Japan, and Southeast Asia
    d. Africa

13. The Los Angeles riots of 1992
    a. were less damaging than the notorious Watts riots
    b. were prompted by increased Mexican and Asian immigration
    c. highlighted the growing income gap, lack of urban policy, and racism in America
    d. were entirely gang related

14. In the early 1980s the Reagan policies toward the former Soviet Union included all of the following EXCEPT
    a. increasing the military budget and nuclear superiority
    b. pushing ahead with the "Star Wars" defensive shield
    c. attacking the USSR as the "evil empire"
    d. withdrawing missiles from Western Europe

15. The "contras" were
    a. counterrevolutionary forces supported by the United States in Nicaragua
    b. counterrevolutionary terrorist forces in El Salvador
    c. Sandinista supporters in Nicaragua
    d. Iranian terrorists who seized the American embassy

16. As history moved into the mid-1990s, the American people faced
    a. a transformed world of international relations
    b. a rapidly changing demographic picture at home
    c. lowered expectations of economic success
    d. all of the above

Essays

1. Assess the achievements and failures of the Reagan, Bush and Clinton administrations in both domestic and foreign policy.

2. Identify and analyze what you think have been the three or four most profoundly significant changes affecting the lives of the American people in the past 50 years.

3. Identify and analyze what you think have been the three or four most significant continuities in the lives of the American people that still remain in our lives today.

ANSWERS TO SAMPLE TEST AND EXAMINATION QUESTIONS*

	Chapter 17		Chapter 18		Chapter 19
1.	a	1.	b	1.	c
2.	d	2.	a	2.	a
3.	c	3.	d	3.	c
4.	a	4.	c	4.	c
5.	a	5.	c	5.	d
6.	b	6.	d	6.	b
7.	b	7.	a	7.	d
8.	a	8.	a	8.	b
9.	c	9.	c	9.	c
10.	b	10.	d	10.	a
11.	c	11.	a	11.	b
12.	b	12.	c	12.	a
13.	a	13.	c	13.	c
14.	d	14.	b	14.	b
15.	c	15.	d	15.	a
16.	b				
17.	a				

	Chapter 20		Chapter 21		Chapter 22		Chapter 23
1.	a	1.	b	1.	d	1.	c
2.	c	2.	d	2.	c	2.	a
3.	c	3.	d	3.	b	3.	d
4.	a	4.	b	4.	a	4.	c
5.	d	5.	d	5.	c	5.	c
6.	c	6.	d	6.	b	6.	c
7.	d	7.	c	7.	b	7.	c
8.	d	8.	b	8.	b	8.	b
9.	c	9.	c	9.	d	9.	d
10.	c	10.	c	10.	a	10.	a
11.	a	11.	a	11.	c	11.	d
12.	a	12.	a	12.	d	12.	d
13.	c	13.	c	13.	b	13.	a
14.	c	14.	a	14.	c	14.	c
15.	d	15.	c	15.	a	15.	b

Answers to the Quotation and Chart Identifications and the Map Questions are found at the end of this section.

Chapter 24

Alphabet Soup

1. b
2. c   ICC: Interstate Commerce Commission
3. c   AAA: Agricultural Adjustment Act
4. d   CIO: Congress of Industrial Organizations
5. a   NIRA: National Industrial Recovery Act (Administration)
6. d   NAACP: National Association for the Advancement of Colored
7. c   People
8. a   CCC: Civilian Conservation Corps
9. b   FERA: Federal Emergency Relief Administration
10. b   TVA: Tennessee Valley Authority
11. b   NLRB: National Labor Relations Board
12. d   FDIC: Federal Deposit Insurance Corporation
13. b
14. b
15. b

Chapter 25	Chapter 26	Chapter 27 Multiple Choice	Matching
1. c	1. a	1. d	1. d
2. a	2. c	2. c	2. f
3. c	3. d	3. b	3. h
4. d	4. b	4. c	4. c
5. d	5. d	5. b	5. a
6. c	6. c	6. c	6. e
7. b	7. c	7. c	7. b
8. a	8. d	8. d	8. g
9. a	9. a	9. c	
10. c	10. d	10. b	
11. d	11. b	11. b	
12. d	12. d	12. a	
13. b	13. c	13. d	
14. c	14. c	14. b	
15. D	15. d	15. a	

Chapter 28	Chapter 29		Chapter 30
	Multiple Choice	Matching	
1. c	1. b	1. j	1. c
2. c	2. d	2. f	2. d
3. c	3. d	3. e	3. a
4. d	4. b	4. h	4. b
5. b	5. d	5. i	5. a
6. c	6. b	6. g	6. d
7. d	7. b	7. c	7. a
8. b	8. c	8. b	8. d
9. b	9. d	9. d	9. c
10. a	10. c	10. a	10. b
11. b	11. a		11. d
12. c	12. a		12. a
13. d	13. b		13. c
14. d	14. a		14. d
15. c	15. c		15. a
			16. d

ANSWERS: IDENTIFY AND INTERPRET:
QUOTATIONS AND CHARTS

Chapter 17 - Quotation

Booker T. Washington, Atlanta Exposition Address, 1895. This speech solidified the Tuskegee educator as the leading black spokesman of a moderate race policy. Washington's emphasis on black economic self-help and his over-cautious position on equal rights endeared him to whites but led to the expression of more assertive policies by other black leaders, most notably by Dr. W. E. B. Du Bois.

Chapter 18 - Chart: White Fertility Rates

1. The chart portrays changes in white fertility rates between 1800 and 1910. Overall, the average white woman bore about half as many children in 1910 as in 1800. Large families were not the rule for white Americans in the latter half of the nineteenth century.

2. The factors lying behind this decline are subtle and debated by historians. As a whole, the pattern points to the fact that Americans were limiting family size (with methods ranging from abortion to abstinence). New norms for family life and child care doubtless played an important part in encouraging families to have fewer children while the belief that women were naturally pure and passionless may well have limited sexual contact between husbands and wives.

3. Overall, the declining fertility of white women points to the growing complexity of American life. As American society became increasingly urban and industrial, large families seemed less desirable than they once had been. Middle-class families (especially those in urban areas) no longer expected their children to make economic contributions to family life and recognized the economic and emotional challenges children presented. New norms also emphasized that fewer was better by insisting that every child deserved a mother's care and attention. The growth of the common school system provides further evidence of the concern Americans had about preparing their children for adult life. The chart also suggests that American white women had fewer demands on their time as family size decreased and helps to explain the growing involvement of women in activities outside the home.

Chapter 20 - Quotation

Theodore Roosevelt in a presidential address stating the Roosevelt Corollary to the Monroe Doctrine, 1904. Roosevelt's police power policy, often employed in the twentieth century, established the pattern of intervention by the United States in the affairs of Central American and Caribbean countries.

Chapter 21 - Chart: Disorderly Tenements

1. In this chart we can see the numbers and selected characteristics of the occupants of 29 disorderly tenement houses in five New York neighborhoods during the first four months of 1909. Although the chart shows that the East Side had the most disorderly tenements, it is not clear whether all the disorderly buildings in each neighborhood are listed or not. Thus we cannot conclude from this chart that the East Side was necessarily the most disorderly area of the city. But we can note that the tenements on the East Side were the most crowded of those described while the buildings in Brooklyn were the least. The chart also dramatizes the ethnic hodgepodge of urban living arrangements. If the nationalities are listed in order of importance, we can suggest that each neighborhood had a distinctive ethnic character. The new immigrants colored life on the East Side while the old immigrants defined the neighborhood between West 104th Street and West 153rd Street.

2. New urban arrangements, immigration patterns, living conditions, and the progressive interest in studying social problems explain this census. The title of the publication from which this chart is drawn suggests the progressive concern for prostitution, conventionally called the social evil.

3. The chart demonstrates the progressive faith in study (especially statistical study) as the basis for reform as well as the progressive zeal for teaching middle-class values to the new immigrants. Moreover, the chart highlights the heterogeneous character of American urban life.

Chapter 22 - Quotation

Women's suffrage, the Nineteenth Amendment to the Constitution, 1920, the fulfillment of a long struggle initiated at Seneca Falls in 1848. The amendment, however, fails to address economic, psychosexual, and other women's rights issues.

Chapter 24 - Quotation

Franklin D. Roosevelt, Inaugural Address, March 4, 1933. Roosevelt gave immediate notice that he would take a strong, activist role in combating the Depression, thus heralding the flurry of executive and congressional reforms of the First Hundred Days of the New Deal.

Chapter 25 - Cartoon

The cartoon shows that after playing a vital role in the wartime economy, women were not, as men wanted, going to be easily squeezed back into a narrow domestic role as homemakers.

Chapter 27 - Quotation

John Foster Dulles, secretary of state under President Eisenhower, A Statement of Policy, 1954. Without saying so directly, Dulles poses the threat of using nuclear weapons rather than conventional forces in resisting Communist aggression, thus escalating the nuclear arms race.

Chapter 27 - Chart: Defense Spending

1. Here we see the pattern of defense expenditures between 1945 and 1960. Defense spending declined rapidly after World War II and began to rise sharply in 1950. Expenditures peaked at $50 billion during the Korean War but remained above $40 billion for the rest of the period.

2. The end of World War II and the emergence of the Cold War explain the pattern of expenditures. The low level of defense spending between 1945 and 1950 suggests, however, that the administration did not easily convince Congress of the need to increase spending dramatically to fight the Cold War. The Korean War is a watershed. Thereafter there seems to have been consensus that high defense spending was necessary.

3. The notable points you might make about this chart include the emergence of a foreign policy consensus by the 1950s, the important contribution defense spending made to national prosperity of that decade, the growth of what Eisenhower called the military-industrial complex, and the emergence of an international arms race, all of which has increased in the years since 1960.

Chapter 29 - Quotations

Martin Luther King, Jr., Letter from Birmingham Jail, 1963. Influenced by both Christianity and Mahatma Gandhi, King's eloquent letter has become a classic statement of the philosophy of nonviolent civil disobedience.

Vilunya Diskin and Wendy Coppedge Sanford, from the Preface to *Our Bodies, Ourselves: A Book by and for Women*, 1973. A product of the Boston Women's Health Book Collective, *Our Bodies, Ourselves* and its various revised versions have had an incalculable influence on women in America.